· TRIPLE TESTED ·
FOR YOUR SUCCESS EVERY TIME

Mum's roast dinner... its smell and its taste so imprinted on our memory that the words alone can arouse our tastebuds like nothing else. And while we cook a far wider range of foods than did our mother, our repertoire still stars lamb as a pivotal player. So versatile, delectable and amenable is this meat that it features in all of the world's great cuisines — for the best lamb recipes ever, turn the page and breathe deeply.

Pamela Clark

FOOD EDITOR

The Great Lamb Cookbook

Contents

4
Quick, easy and delicious

Until now, a quick and easy lamb recipe translated into grilling a few chops — here is a sampler of more than 50 exciting yet simple inducements to help motivate you into expanding the brief. Many of these delicious recipes can be prepared ahead so that, come mealtime, all that's left to do is add a few finishing touches, sit back and take the credit.

Lamb and cashew stir-fry, page 35

Lamb with lemons and olives, page 44

Cajun cutlets with cucumber salsa, page 4

Lamb and quince tagine, page 84

Lamb....

Light, luscious, lean and loved by everyone who's ever tasted it. And you can't go past lamb for its sheer versatility and adaptability to a wide spectrum of menus and individual recipes. Its sweet taste and delicate texture make lamb truly one of the most popular meats throughout the world.

BRITISH & NORTH AMERICAN READERS:
Please note that Australian cup and spoon measurements are metric. A quick conversion guide appears on page 118. A glossary explaining unfamiliar terms and ingredients begins on page 112.

Quick, easy and delicious

◧ The super recipes on these pages fill the bill when you have so much else on your plate, you hardly have time to add food to it! Simple, exciting and more consumable than consuming, these clever ideas are light years away from the humble grilled chop we so often resort to when time's of the essence. Best of all, many can be made ahead and given a swift, spectacular finishing touch that's expressly your own.

CAJUN CUTLETS WITH CUCUMBER SALSA

12 lamb cutlets
2 teaspoons ground cumin
2 teaspoons ground coriander
1 teaspoon ground turmeric
1 teaspoon sweet paprika
1 teaspoon ground oregano
1 teaspoon chilli powder
1/2 teaspoon ground clove
2 tablespoons olive oil

CUCUMBER SALSA
2 (260g) Lebanese cucumbers, seeded, chopped
2 medium (260g) tomatoes, seeded, chopped
1 medium (200g) yellow capsicum, seeded, chopped
2 green onions, chopped finely
1 tablespoon balsamic vinegar
1 tablespoon olive oil

Coat lamb with combined spices and oil in large bowl; cover, refrigerate 30 minutes. *[Can be made ahead to this stage. Cover; refrigerate overnight or freeze.]*

Cook lamb, in batches, on heated oiled griddle (or grill or barbecue) until browned on both sides and cooked as desired. Serve with Cucumber Salsa.

Cucumber Salsa Combine all ingredients in small bowl; refrigerate, covered, 30 minutes.

SERVES 4

Plate from The Bay Tree Kitchen Shop

Plates from Accoutrement; napkin from Ruby Star Traders

FRENCH-ONION BAKED CHUMP CHOPS

2 tablespoons olive oil
12 lamb chump chops
6 baby (150g) onions, halved
2 cloves garlic, crushed
2 small (400g) leeks, chopped
40g packet French onion soup mix
1 1/2 cups (375ml) boiling water
1 tablespoon finely chopped fresh parsley

Heat half the oil in large flameproof baking dish; cook lamb, in batches, until browned both sides. Heat remaining oil in same dish; cook onion, garlic and leek, stirring, until onion is browned lightly.

Return lamb to dish; sprinkle with soup mix, pour over water. Bake, covered, in moderate oven 40 minutes. Uncover; bake about 30 minutes or until lamb is tender and sauce thickened. [Best made on day of serving.] Just before serving, sprinkle with parsley.

SERVES 4 TO 6

KIBBE-BURGERS WITH MINTED CREME FRAICHE

1/4 cup (40g) burghul
500g minced lamb
1 medium (150g) onion, chopped finely
2 cloves garlic, crushed
1/4 cup (40g) chopped toasted pine nuts
2 teaspoons ground cumin
2 teaspoons mixed spice
1/2 teaspoon ground cinnamon
2 tablespoons chopped fresh parsley
1/3 cup chopped fresh mint leaves
1 tablespoon olive oil
1 long loaf Turkish pide
1 (130g) Lebanese cucumber
1 medium (120g) carrot
1 small radicchio
3/4 cup (180ml) creme fraiche
2 tablespoons lemon juice
1/2 teaspoon cracked black pepper

Cover burghul with cold water in small bowl, stand 15 minutes; drain. Rinse burghul under cold water; drain, squeeze out excess moisture. Combine burghul in large bowl with lamb, onion, garlic, nuts, spices, parsley and half the mint; shape lamb mixture into 4 patties. [Can be made ahead to this stage. Cover; refrigerate overnight or freeze.]

Heat oil in large pan; cook patties, uncovered, until browned both sides and cooked as desired.

Meanwhile, quarter pide; split each piece horizontally, toast both sides. Using a vegetable peeler, cut cucumber and carrot into long, thin strips. Trim and tear radicchio into pieces. Combine remaining ingredients in small jug. Layer patties, cucumber, carrot and radicchio on toast; drizzle with minted creme fraiche, top with toast.

SERVES 4

Above French-onion baked chump chops
Right Kibbe-burgers with minted creme fraiche

Bowl from The Home Store; fork from Villeroy & Boch

FETTUCCINE WITH LAMB, CAPSICUM AND PEPITAS

2 medium (400g) red capsicums
20g butter
¹/₃ cup (55g) pepitas
1 cup (250ml) tomato puree
2 cloves garlic, crushed
1¹/₄ cups (310ml) beef stock
**1 tablespoon chopped fresh
   tarragon leaves**
1 teaspoon ground cumin
600g lamb eye of loin
2 teaspoons salt
1 teaspoon cracked black pepper
2 tablespoons olive oil
500g fettuccine

Quarter capsicums, remove seeds and membranes. Roast under grill or in very hot oven, skin-side up, until skin blisters and blackens. Cover capsicum pieces in plastic or paper for 5 minutes, peel away skin; slice into 1cm pieces.

Heat butter in medium pan; cook pepitas, stirring, about 3 minutes or until pepitas pop. Drain on absorbent paper.

Combine puree, garlic, stock, tarragon and cumin in large pan. Bring to boil; simmer, uncovered, 5 minutes or until sauce thickens slightly. *[Can be made ahead to this stage. Cover capsicum, pepitas and sauce separately; refrigerate overnight or freeze.]*

Place lamb in large bowl; sprinkle with combined salt and pepper. Heat oil in large pan; cook lamb, uncovered, until browned all over and cooked as desired. Cover lamb, stand 5 minutes; slice thinly.

Meanwhile, cook fettuccine in large pan of boiling water, uncovered, until just tender; drain. Gently toss fettuccine in large bowl with lamb, capsicum, pepitas and hot tomato sauce.

SERVES 4

LOIN CHOPS WITH CAFE DE PARIS BUTTER

12 lamb loin chops
$1/2$ cup (125ml)
 Worcestershire sauce
1 tablespoon lemon juice
1 clove garlic, crushed
2 tablespoons drained
 baby capers
1 tablespoon finely chopped
 fresh chives
2 tablespoons finely chopped
 fresh parsley
1 teaspoon finely grated
 fresh ginger
250g butter, softened

Place lamb in large bowl with $1/3$ cup of the Worcestershire sauce, toss lamb to coat with sauce; cover, refrigerate 1 hour.

Blend or process all the remaining ingredients until smooth. Using plastic wrap as a guide, roll butter mixture into log shape; wrap in oiled foil, refrigerate until firm. *[Can be made ahead to this stage. Cover lamb; refrigerate, separately, overnight or freeze.]*

Cook lamb, in batches, on heated oiled griddle (or grill or barbecue) until browned both sides and cooked as desired; serve with sliced chilled butter.

SERVES 4

Opposite Fettuccine with lamb, capsicum and pepitas
Left Loin chops with cafe de Paris butter

THAI LAMB COCONUT SOUP

2 tablespoons peanut oil
1 medium (150g) onion, sliced
2 cloves garlic, crushed
2 teaspoons finely grated
    fresh ginger
1 tablespoon finely chopped
    fresh lemon grass
6 fresh curry leaves
2 tablespoons green curry paste
2 medium (400g) potatoes,
    chopped coarsely
1 litre (4 cups) chicken stock
3 cups (750ml) coconut milk
1 tablespoon fish sauce
1/4 cup (60ml) lime juice
500g lamb eye of loin
4 green onions, sliced thinly
1 cup (80g) bean sprouts

LAMB AND LEEK FRITTATA

1 tablespoon olive oil
3 cloves garlic, crushed
500g minced lamb
2 tablespoons Worcestershire sauce
2 tablespoons balsamic vinegar
2 tablespoons tomato paste
20g butter
1 large (500g) leek, sliced thinly
2 medium (800g) kumara,
    chopped coarsely
1 1/4 cups (150g) coarsely grated
    cheddar cheese
4 eggs
300ml cream
1/3 cup (80ml) sour cream

Heat oil in large pan; cook garlic and lamb, stirring, until lamb is browned and cooked through. Add sauce, vinegar and paste; cook, stirring, about 5 minutes or until sauce thickens. Place in large bowl; cover to keep warm.

Heat butter in same pan; cook leek, stirring, until soft. Remove from heat; cover to keep warm.

Boil, steam or microwave kumara until tender; drain. Place kumara in separate large bowl; mash.

Press leek onto base of oiled deep 19cm square cake pan; top with mince mixture, then mashed kumara. Sprinkle with cheese.

Whisk eggs, cream and sour cream in medium bowl; pour over frittata mixture, stand 5 minutes. Bake, uncovered, in moderate oven about 45 minutes or until frittata is set and top browned. *[Can be made ahead to this stage. Cover; refrigerate overnight.]*

SERVES 4 TO 6

Above Lamb and leek frittata
Right Thai lamb coconut soup
Far right Lamb and macadamia nut salad

Heat half the oil in large pan; cook onion, garlic, ginger, lemon grass and curry leaves, stirring, until onion is soft. Add curry paste; cook, stirring, until fragrant.

Add potatoes, stock, milk, sauce and juice. Bring to boil; simmer, covered, about 30 minutes or until potatoes are tender. Discard curry leaves; blend or process soup mixture until almost smooth. Return to pan; cover to keep warm. *[Can be made ahead to this stage. Cover; refrigerate overnight or freeze.]*

Heat remaining oil in separate large pan; cook lamb, uncovered, until browned all over and cooked as desired. Stand lamb 5 minutes; slice thinly.

Stir lamb, green onion and sprouts into hot soup mixture just before serving.

SERVES 4 TO 6

Platter from The Home Store; cutlery from Villeroy & Boch

Tray and bowl from Olson & Blake Collectables

LAMB AND MACADAMIA NUT SALAD

500g lamb eye of loin
1/4 cup (60ml) dry red wine
2 cloves garlic, crushed
4 large (360g) egg tomatoes, quartered
1 tablespoon olive oil
1/2 teaspoon sugar
1/2 teaspoon freshly ground black pepper
1/4 cup (60ml) red wine vinegar
1 teaspoon Dijon mustard
1 clove garlic, chopped coarsely
1/4 cup (20g) coarsely grated parmesan cheese
1/4 cup (60ml) macadamia oil
1 tablespoon chopped fresh basil leaves
1/2 cup (75g) macadamia nuts, toasted, chopped
250g rocket, trimmed

Combine lamb, wine and crushed garlic in large bowl; cover, refrigerate 30 minutes. *[Can be made ahead to this stage. Cover; refrigerate overnight or freeze.]*

Place tomatoes on oven tray; drizzle with olive oil, sprinkle with sugar and pepper. Bake, uncovered, in moderate oven about 10 minutes or until tomatoes are soft.

Drain lamb; reserve marinade. Cook lamb, uncovered, in large heated oiled pan until browned all over and cooked as desired. Cover lamb, stand for 5 minutes; slice thinly.

Add marinade to same pan; bring to boil. Simmer, uncovered, until reduced to 1 tablespoon; blend or process with vinegar, mustard, chopped garlic, cheese, macadamia oil and basil until smooth.

Gently toss lamb, tomatoes, nuts and and rocket in large bowl with dressing.

SERVES 4

LAMB, FENNEL AND CORN SALAD

500g lamb eye of loin
1 teaspoon Seasoned Pepper
1 (500g) fennel bulb
2 (800g) corn cobs
50g snow pea sprouts
2 medium (240g) carrots, sliced thinly

¹/₃ cup (80ml) white wine vinegar
¹/₃ cup (80ml) peanut oil
1 clove garlic, crushed
2 teaspoons sugar
1 tablespoon lime juice
2 tablespoons chopped fresh dill leaves

Sprinkle lamb with Seasoned Pepper; cook on heated oiled griddle (or grill or barbecue) until browned all over and cooked as desired. Cover lamb, stand for 5 minutes; slice thinly.

Trim fennel, cut bulb into thin slices. Cut kernels from corn; boil, steam or microwave kernels until just tender. Gently toss lamb, fennel and corn in large bowl with sprouts, carrots and combined remaining ingredients. *[Best made on day of serving.]*

SERVES 4

SPAGHETTI WITH LAMB, FETTA AND ARTICHOKES

8 small (480g) egg tomatoes
2 tablespoons olive oil
1 tablespoon balsamic vinegar
2 cloves garlic, halved
500g lamb eye of loin
20g butter
2 cups (140g) stale breadcrumbs
2 cloves garlic, crushed
250g spaghetti
¹/₂ cup (80g) black olives, seeded
1 cup (200g) crumbled fetta cheese
400g can artichoke hearts in oil,
   drained, quartered

Halve tomatoes lengthways; place, cut-side up, in large baking dish, drizzle with half the oil. Bake, uncovered, in very hot oven about 20 minutes or until soft. Blend or process tomatoes, remaining oil, vinegar and halved garlic until pureed. *[Can be made ahead to this stage. Cover; refrigerate overnight or freeze.]*

Cook lamb in large heated oiled pan, uncovered, until browned all over and cooked as desired. Cover lamb, stand for 5 minutes; slice thinly.

Meanwhile, heat butter in same large pan; cook breadcrumbs and crushed garlic, stirring, until browned lightly and crisp.

Cook pasta in large pan of boiling water, uncovered, until just tender; drain. Gently toss hot pasta and lamb in large bowl with olives, cheese and artichokes; top with hot tomato puree, sprinkle with breadcrumb mixture.

SERVES 4 TO 6

Opposite Lamb, fennel and corn salad
Below Spaghetti with lamb, fetta and artichokes

SAUSAGES WITH HERBED RISOTTO

1 litre (4 cups) lamb or beef stock
2 cups (500ml) vegetable stock
1 cup (250ml) dry red wine
2 tablespoons olive oil
4 (560g) lamb sausages
30g butter
3 cloves garlic, crushed
1 large (200g) onion, chopped
2 cups (400g) arborio rice
1/2 cup (60g) grated cheddar cheese
1/3 cup (25g) grated parmesan cheese
2 tablespoons finely chopped fresh sage leaves
1/4 cup finely chopped fresh mint leaves

Combine stocks and wine in large pan; bring to boil then simmer.

Meanwhile, heat 1 tablespoon of the oil in medium pan; cook sausages, uncovered, until browned all over and cooked through. Remove sausages from pan, drain on absorbent paper; cover to keep warm.

Discard oil in pan; heat remaining oil and butter in same pan. Cook garlic and onion, stirring, until onion is soft. Add rice; stir to coat in butter mixture. Stir in 1 cup hot stock mixture; cook, stirring, over low heat until liquid is absorbed. Continue adding stock mixture, in 1-cup batches, stirring, until absorbed between each addition. Total cooking time should be about 35 minutes or until rice is just tender. Gently stir in sliced sausages, cheeses and leaves. [Best made just before serving.]

SERVES 4

China from Villeroy & Boch; cutlery from The Home Store

GRILLED LAMB PIZZA WITH ROSEMARY VINAIGRETTE

We used large (25cm diameter) packaged pizza bases for this recipe.

8 lamb schnitzels
2 tablespoons Dijon mustard
4 cloves garlic, crushed
1 tablespoon finely chopped
    fresh rosemary
2 tablespoons olive oil
250g button mushrooms, halved
2 x 355g pizza bases
1/2 cup (125ml) bottled tomato
    pasta sauce
3 cups (375g) coarsely grated
    pizza cheese
1/2 cup (30g) sun-dried tomatoes
    in oil, drained
200g baby spinach leaves
1/4 cup (20g) flaked parmesan
    cheese

ROSEMARY VINAIGRETTE
2 tablespoons white wine vinegar
1 tablespoon seeded mustard
1/3 cup (25g) finely grated
    parmesan cheese
2 teaspoons finely chopped
    fresh rosemary
2 cloves garlic, crushed
1/2 cup (125ml) olive oil

Place lamb between sheets of plastic wrap; pound until of an even thickness. Coat lamb with combined mustard, garlic, rosemary and oil in shallow dish; cover, refrigerate 30 minutes. *[Can be made ahead to this stage. Cover; refrigerate overnight or freeze.]*

Cook mushrooms in small heated oiled pan, stirring, about 5 minutes or until browned lightly and tender.

Place pizza bases on oiled oven trays; spread with pasta sauce; sprinkle with pizza cheese, mushrooms and halved tomatoes. Bake, uncovered, in hot oven about 15 minutes or until pizzas are just browned and bases crisp.

Meanwhile, cook lamb on heated oiled griddle (or grill or barbecue) until browned both sides and cooked through.

Gently toss spinach with Rosemary Vinaigrette in large bowl. Place lamb and spinach on pizzas; sprinkle with parmesan.

Rosemary Vinaigrette Combine all ingredients in jar; shake well.

SERVES 4

Plate from The Bay Tree Kitchen Shop

CHILLI LAMB, PAPAYA AND AVOCADO

While frequently known as papaw or pawpaw locally and elsewhere in the world, the correct name for this luscious, juicy, sweet tropical fruit is in fact papaya.

750g lamb eye of loin
2 teaspoons chilli powder
2 teaspoons ground cumin
1 teaspoon ground coriander
1 teaspoon ground ginger
1 small (500g) papaya, chopped
1 large (320g) avocado, chopped
1 medium (170g) red onion,
    chopped finely
2 small fresh red chillies, seeded,
    chopped finely
2 tablespoons lime juice
1 tablespoon chopped fresh
    coriander leaves
1/2 long loaf Turkish pide

Coat lamb with combined spices in large bowl; cover, refrigerate 30 minutes. *[Can be made ahead to this stage. Cover; refrigerate overnight or freeze.]*

Cook lamb, uncovered, in heated oiled pan until browned all over and cooked as desired. Cover lamb, stand 5 minutes; slice thinly.

Combine papaya, avocado, onion, chilli, juice and coriander in large bowl. Quarter pide; split each piece horizontally, toast both sides. Serve sliced lamb with fruit mixture and toast.

SERVES 4 TO 6

Opposite above Sausages with herbed risotto
Opposite Grilled lamb pizza with rosemary vinaigrette
Above Chilli lamb, papaya and avocado

LAMB SALAD NICOISE

2 large pieces pitta
1 tablespoon olive oil
500g lamb eye of loin
150g green beans, trimmed
1 baby cos lettuce
150g curly endive
400g radishes, trimmed,
 sliced thinly
1 medium (170g) red onion, sliced
4 hard-boiled eggs, quartered
8 anchovy fillets in oil, drained

BUTTERMILK DRESSING
1/2 cup (125ml) light olive oil
2 cloves garlic, chopped coarsely
2 tablespoons white wine vinegar
1 teaspoon sugar
2 tablespoons chopped fresh
 basil leaves
1/2 cup (125ml) buttermilk

Place pitta on oven tray; toast, un-covered, in moderately hot oven about 10 minutes or until crisp. Cool pitta; break into pieces.

Heat oil in large pan; cook lamb, uncovered, until browned all over and cooked as desired. Stand lamb, covered, 5 minutes; slice thinly.

Boil, steam or microwave beans until just tender; drain. Rinse under cold water; drain.

Just before serving, gently toss pitta pieces, lamb and beans in large bowl with lettuce, endive, radish, onion, eggs, anchovy fillets and Buttermilk Dressing.

Buttermilk Dressing Blend or process all ingredients until smooth; cover, refrigerate 30 minutes.

SERVES 4 TO 6

Plate from Orson & Blake Collectables

LAMB, PINE NUT, FETTA AND PARSLEY TRIANGLES

700g minced lamb
250g fetta, crumbled
1/3 cup chopped fresh parsley
1 tablespoon sumac
1 tablespoon ground cumin
2 cloves garlic, crushed
2 eggs, beaten
1 teaspoon cracked black pepper
16 sheets fillo pastry
125g butter, melted

Using hands, combine lamb, cheese, parsley, sumac, cumin, garlic, eggs and pepper in large bowl.

To prevent fillo drying out, cover with damp tea-towel until ready to use.

Brush 1 sheet of fillo with some of the butter; fold in half, brush with more butter. Place 1/3 cup lamb mixture in one corner, 1cm in from edge, flatten slightly.

Fold opposite corner of fillo diagonally across the filling to form a large triangle. Continue folding to end of fillo, retaining triangular shape. Repeat with remaining pastry, butter and lamb mixture.

Brush triangles with melted butter; bake, in batches, on lightly oiled oven trays in moderately hot oven about 15 minutes or until browned lightly and cooked through.

MAKES 16

Opposite Lamb salad nicoise
Above Lamb, pine nut, fetta and parsley triangles

KEBABS WITH MINT AND PISTACHIO PESTO

We used lamb cut from the leg for this recipe. Soak bamboo skewers in water overnight to prevent burning.

1kg diced lamb

MINT AND PISTACHIO PESTO
**1 cup firmly packed fresh
   mint leaves**
1/3 cup (50g) pistachios, toasted
**1/3 cup (25g) coarsely grated
   parmesan cheese**
2 cloves garlic, crushed
1 tablespoon lemon juice
1/4 cup (60ml) olive oil
2 tablespoons water, approximately

Thread lamb onto 12 skewers. Cook kebabs, in batches, on heated oiled griddle (or grill or barbecue) until browned all over and cooked as desired. Serve kebabs immediately, with Mint and Pistachio Pesto.

Mint and Pistachio Pesto Blend or process mint, nuts, cheese, garlic and juice until well combined. With motor operating, gradually pour in oil and just enough water to give the desired consistency. *[Can be made ahead to this stage. Cover; refrigerate overnight.]*

SERVES 4 TO 6

GREEK MEATBALLS WITH LEMON YOGURT SAUCE

1kg minced lamb
**1 large (200g) onion,
   chopped finely**
1 egg, beaten
**1/4 cup finely chopped fresh
   mint leaves**
**2 tablespoons finely chopped
   fresh flat-leaf parsley**
**2 tablespoons finely grated
   lemon rind**
1 1/2 tablespoons ground cumin
3 cloves garlic, crushed
1 teaspoon salt
1 teaspoon cracked black pepper

LEMON YOGURT SAUCE
200ml yogurt
**2 tablespoons finely chopped
   fresh mint leaves**
1 1/2 tablespoons lemon juice
1/2 teaspoon sugar

Using hands, combine all ingredients in large bowl. Roll level tablespoons of mixture into balls. Place on tray; cover, refrigerate 30 minutes. *[Can be made ahead to this stage. Cover; refrigerate overnight or freeze.]*

Cook meatballs, in batches, on heated oiled griddle (or grill or barbecue) until browned all over and cooked through.

Serve meatballs immediately with Lemon Yogurt Sauce.

Lemon Yogurt Sauce Combine all ingredients in small bowl; refrigerate 30 minutes.

SERVES 4 TO 6

HOMEMADE LAMB SAUSAGES WITH PENNE

750g minced lamb
1 medium (150g) onion, chopped finely
2 cloves garlic, crushed
2 teaspoons chopped fresh sage leaves
1 egg, beaten
1/2 cup (35g) stale breadcrumbs
2 tablespoons olive oil
1/4 cup (60ml) dry white wine
20g butter
200g button mushrooms, sliced
300ml cream
1 cup (250ml) vegetable stock
2 teaspoons Dijon mustard
250g penne
1/2 cup (40g) coarsely grated parmesan cheese

Using hands, combine lamb, onion, garlic, sage, egg and breadcrumbs in large bowl. Form 1/4 cups of mixture into sausage shapes. Place on tray; cover, refrigerate 30 minutes. *[Can be made ahead to this stage. Cover; refrigerate overnight or freeze.]*

Heat half the oil in large pan; cook sausages, in batches, until browned and cooked through. Cover to keep warm.

Add wine to same pan. Bring to boil; simmer, stirring, until most of the wine has evaporated.

Heat butter with remaining oil in same pan; cook mushrooms, stirring, until just tender. Add cream, stock and mustard; cook, stirring, about 10 minutes or until sauce thickens slightly.

Meanwhile, cook pasta in large pan of boiling water, uncovered, until just tender; drain. Gently toss pasta in large bowl with sausages, sauce and cheese.

SERVES 4 TO 6

Opposite above Kebabs with mint and pistachio pesto
Opposite Greek meatballs with lemon yogurt sauce
Right Homemade lamb sausages with penne

RISOTTO MILANESE WITH LAMB

1 litre (4 cups) lamb or beef stock
1 cup (250ml) dry red wine
1 cup (250ml) water
1/3 cup (80ml) olive oil
500g lamb strips
3 cloves garlic, crushed
1 large (200g) onion,
** chopped finely**
200g Swiss brown mushrooms,
** sliced thinly**
1/2 teaspoon saffron threads
2 cups (400g) arborio rice
1/2 cup (60g) coarsely grated
** cheddar cheese**

CREAMED MUSHROOM SAUCE
20g butter
200g button mushrooms, sliced
1 1/2 tablespoons lemon juice
300ml cream

Combine stock, wine and water in large pan; bring to boil then simmer.

Meanwhile, heat half the oil in medium pan; cook lamb, in batches, stirring until browned all over and cooked through. Cover to keep warm.

Heat remaining oil in same pan; cook garlic, onion, mushrooms and saffron, stirring, until onion is soft. Add rice, stir to coat in oil mixture. Stir in 1 cup hot stock mixture; cook, stirring, over low heat until liquid is absorbed. Continue adding stock mixture, in 1-cup batches, stirring, until absorbed between each addition. Total cooking time should be about 35 minutes or until rice is just tender. Gently stir in lamb and cheese; serve with Creamed Mushroom Sauce.

Creamed Mushroom Sauce Heat butter in medium pan; cook mushrooms, stirring, until browned. Stir in juice and cream. Bring to boil; simmer, stirring, about 3 minutes or until sauce thickens slightly.

SERVES 4

CUMIN-CRUSTED LAMB WITH GAZPACHO SAUCE

Gazpacho is traditionally a cold Spanish soup made primarily of cucumber and tomato; we've taken out some of the liquid but none of the flavour with this delectable sauce.

1 tablespoon cumin seeds
2 teaspoons ground cumin
2 tablespoons plain flour
750g lamb eye of loin
1/3 cup (80ml) olive oil
4 slices white bread
1 clove garlic, crushed

GAZPACHO SAUCE
2 medium (380g) tomatoes,
** seeded, chopped**
1 (130g) Lebanese cucumber,
** seeded, chopped**
1 small (100g) red onion, chopped
2 tablespoons lime juice
1 teaspoon sugar
1/4 teaspoon Tabasco sauce
1/4 cup (60ml) tomato juice

Combine cumin seeds, ground cumin and flour in small bowl. Brush lamb with a little of the oil; press on cumin mixture. *[Can be made ahead to this stage. Cover; refrigerate overnight.]*

Heat half the remaining oil in large pan; cook lamb, uncovered, until browned all over and cooked as desired. Cover lamb, stand 5 minutes; slice thinly.

Trim crusts from bread; cut bread into 2cm squares. Heat remaining oil in pan; cook bread and garlic, stirring, until browned lightly and crisp.

Serve lamb with fried bread squares and Gazpacho Sauce.

Gazpacho Sauce Combine all ingredients in medium bowl; cover, refrigerate 30 minutes.

SERVES 4

Opposite Risotto Milanese with lamb
Above Cumin-crusted lamb with gazpacho sauce

LAMB AND VEGETABLE FREE-FORM PIE

2 tablespoons olive oil
1 medium (150g) onion, chopped
2 cloves garlic, crushed
750g minced lamb
400g can tomatoes
2 tablespoons tomato paste
1/4 cup (60ml) dry red wine
1/4 cup (60ml) tomato sauce
1 tablespoon Worcestershire sauce
1/2 cup (125ml) vegetable stock
150g button mushrooms, sliced
250g spinach leaves, trimmed
2 sheets ready-rolled puff pastry

1 egg, beaten
1/2 teaspoon caraway seeds
1/2 teaspoon sesame seeds
1/2 teaspoon poppy seeds

Heat half the oil in large pan; cook onion and garlic, stirring, until onion is soft. Add lamb; cook, stirring, until browned and cooked through. Add undrained crushed tomatoes, paste, wine, sauces and stock. Bring to boil; simmer, uncovered, about 20 minutes or until most of the liquid evaporates. [Can be made ahead to this stage. Cover; refrigerate overnight or freeze.] Heat remaining oil in separate small pan; cook mushrooms, stirring, until browned and tender. Boil, steam or microwave spinach until just wilted; rinse under cold water, drain. Squeeze out excess moisture; spread spinach on absorbent paper.

Cut 24cm round from each pastry sheet. Place 1 round on oiled oven tray; top with lamb mixture, leaving 2cm border. Top lamb with mushrooms and spinach. Brush around border with egg; cover with remaining pastry round. Press edges together; brush pie with egg, sprinkle with combined seeds. Make shallow cuts in top; bake, uncovered, in hot oven about 35 minutes or until top is browned and pie is heated through.

SERVES 4 TO 6

White plate from The Bay Tree Kitchen Shop

SWEET AND SOUR LAMB CHOPS

1 tablespoon vegetable oil
1 large (200g) onion, sliced
1 medium (200g) red capsicum, chopped
1 medium (200g) yellow capsicum, chopped
2 tablespoons soy sauce
2 tablespoons tomato sauce
2 tablespoons brown sugar
1/3 cup (80ml) white vinegar
450g can pineapple pieces in natural juice
6 green onions, sliced
1 tablespoon cornflour
1 cup (250ml) water
8 lamb chump chops

Heat oil in medium pan; cook onion and capsicum, stirring, until onion is browned lightly. Stir in sauces, sugar, vinegar, undrained pineapple, green onion and blended cornflour and water. Bring to boil; cook, stirring, about 5 minutes or until sweet and sour mixture thickens. *[Can be made ahead to this stage. Cover; refrigerate overnight.]*

Cook lamb, in batches, in large heated oiled pan, until browned both sides and cooked as desired. Serve sweet and sour mixture over lamb.

SERVES 4

Opposite Lamb and vegetable free-form pie
Above Sweet and sour lamb chops

STRAW POTATO AND LAMB SALAD

1/4 cup (60ml) lemon juice
2 tablespoons olive oil
1/4 cup (60ml) balsamic vinegar
2 cloves garlic, crushed
3 teaspoons brown sugar
2 teaspoons chopped fresh thyme
500g lamb eye of loin
1 tablespoon balsamic
    vinegar, extra
2 medium (400g) potatoes
vegetable oil, for shallow frying
50g hot salami, sliced thinly
1 baby cos lettuce, trimmed, torn
1 medium (170g) red onion, sliced
250g cherry tomatoes, halved
50g snow pea sprouts

Whisk juice, olive oil, vinegar, garlic, sugar and thyme together in small bowl; refrigerate two-thirds of the dressing, covered, in separate small bowl.

Combine lamb and extra vinegar with remaining dressing in shallow dish;

China and napkin from Accoutrement

LAMB AND ROAST VEGETABLE STACK

2 medium (400g) red capsicums
1 medium (120g) yellow
    zucchini, sliced
1 medium (120g) green
    zucchini, sliced
2 tablespoons olive oil
1 medium (170g) red onion, sliced
400g lamb strips
1 long loaf Turkish pide

AVOCADO CREAM
2 medium (500g) avocados, chopped
2 tablespoons horseradish cream
2 tablespoons lemon juice

Quarter capsicums, remove seeds and membranes. Roast under grill or in very hot oven, skin-side up, until skin blisters and blackens. Cover capsicum pieces in plastic or paper for 5 minutes, peel away skin; slice thickly.

Brush zucchini slices with half the oil; cook, in batches, on heated oiled griddle (or grill or barbecue) until browned and tender. *[Can be made ahead to this stage. Cover, separately; refrigerate overnight.]*

Meanwhile, heat remaining oil in large pan; cook onion, stirring, until soft. Add lamb; cook, stirring, until browned all over and cooked as desired. Quarter pide; split each piece horizontally, toast both sides. Spread 4 pieces toasted pide with some of the Avocado Cream; divide lamb mixture and roasted vegetables among the 4 stacks. Top each of the stacks with remaining Avocado Cream and remaining 4 pieces toasted pide.

Avocado Cream Blend or process all ingredients until smooth.

SERVES 4

Above Lamb and roast vegetable stack
Right Straw potato and lamb salad
Far right Lamb with chermoulla and lemon couscous

cover, refrigerate several hours or overnight. *[Can also be frozen, covered, at this stage.]*

Drain lamb; discard marinade. Cook lamb on heated oiled griddle (or grill or barbecue) until browned all over and cooked as desired. Cover lamb, stand 5 minutes; slice thinly.

Meanwhile, cut peeled potatoes into 2mm slices; cut slices lengthways in 2mm strips. Rinse potato under cold water until water runs clear; drain, pat dry with absorbent paper.

Heat vegetable oil in deep medium pan; shallow-fry salami, in batches, until crisp. Drain on absorbent paper; break into small pieces.

Reheat same oil; shallow-fry potato, in batches, until golden-brown and crisp. Gently toss lamb, salami and half the potato straws in large bowl with lettuce, onion, tomatoes, sprouts and remaining dressing; scatter over remaining potato.

SERVES 4

Plate from The Bay Tree Kitchen Shop

LAMB WITH CHERMOULLA AND LEMON COUSCOUS

2 tablespoons grated lemon rind
2 cloves garlic, chopped coarsely
2 small fresh red chillies, seeded, chopped coarsely
1 tablespoon grated fresh ginger
1/4 cup chopped fresh flat-leaf parsley
1/4 cup chopped fresh coriander leaves
1 teaspoon sweet paprika
1/4 cup (60ml) olive oil
8 lamb forequarter chops

LEMON COUSCOUS

1 1/2 cups (300g) couscous
1 1/2 cups (375ml) boiling water
1/3 cup (25g) flaked almonds, toasted
1 tablespoon finely grated lemon rind

1 tablespoon lemon juice
2 tablespoons chopped fresh coriander leaves
40g butter

Blend or process rind, garlic, chilli, ginger, herbs, paprika and oil. Place lamb in single layer in shallow dish; coat lamb in chermoulla paste. Cover; refrigerate 3 hours or overnight. *[Can also be frozen, covered, at this stage.]*

Cook lamb, in batches, on heated oiled griddle (or grill or barbecue) until browned both sides and cooked as desired. Serve with Lemon Couscous.

Lemon Couscous Combine couscous and water in large bowl; cover, stand about 5 minutes or until water is absorbed. Stir in almonds, rind, juice and coriander.

Heat butter in large pan, add couscous mixture; cook, stirring, about 5 minutes or until heated through.

SERVES 4

LAMB PATTIES WITH TOMATO AND OREGANO SALSA

800g minced lamb

1/2 cup (60g) seeded black olives, chopped finely

100g pancetta, chopped finely

2 tablespoons chopped fresh oregano

1 tablespoon Dijon mustard

1 tablespoon tomato paste

1 teaspoon cracked black pepper

TOMATO AND OREGANO SALSA

1 medium (250g) avocado, chopped finely

2 medium (380g) tomatoes, chopped finely

2 teaspoons finely chopped fresh oregano

1 tablespoon lemon juice

1 tablespoon olive oil

1 teaspoon balsamic vinegar

Using hands, combine all ingredients in large bowl; shape mixture into 8 patties. Place on tray; cover, refrigerate 30 minutes. *[Can be made ahead to this stage. Cover; refrigerate overnight or freeze.]*

Cook patties, in batches, on heated oiled griddle (or grill or barbecue) until browned both sides and cooked through; serve with Tomato and Oregano Salsa.

Tomato and Oregano Salsa Combine all ingredients in small bowl.

SERVES 4

SOUR-SWEET MEATBALLS WITH RED LENTILS

400g minced lamb

1 tablespoon tamarind paste

2 teaspoons finely chopped fresh lemon grass

3 cups (750ml) lamb or beef stock

1 cup (200g) red lentils

2 tablespoons olive oil

4 cloves garlic, crushed

1 medium (150g) onion, chopped finely

1 teaspoon finely grated fresh ginger

2 medium (380g) tomatoes, chopped coarsely

1/4 teaspoon cayenne pepper

LAMB WITH EGGPLANT CREAM AND WINE SAUCE

2 large (1kg) eggplants
3 cloves garlic, chopped coarsely
2 tablespoons olive oil
1 tablespoon lime juice
2 tablespoons coarsely chopped fresh basil leaves
8 lamb chump chops
20g butter
1 large (200g) onion, sliced
2 cloves garlic, crushed
1 tablespoon brown sugar
1/4 cup (60ml) dry red wine
3/4 cup (180ml) lamb or beef stock

Pierce unpeeled eggplants several times with skewer. Place whole eggplants on oiled oven tray; bake, uncovered, in hot oven about 30 minutes or until soft and slightly charred. Halve each eggplant lengthways; place, flesh-side down, on wire rack in shallow baking dish. Drain eggplant about 30 minutes or until liquid runs out; discard liquid. Peel eggplant, discard skin; chop flesh roughly. Blend or process eggplant with chopped garlic, oil, juice and basil until smooth. [Can be made ahead to this stage. Cover; refrigerate overnight or freeze.]

Cook lamb in large heated oiled pan, in batches, until browned both sides and cooked as desired. Cover to keep warm.

Heat butter in same pan; cook onion and crushed garlic, stirring, until onion is browned lightly. Add sugar and wine; cook, stirring, until wine is almost evaporated. Add stock. Bring to boil; simmer, uncovered, about 3 minutes or until sauce thickens slightly. Serve lamb with eggplant cream and wine sauce.

SERVES 4

Opposite Lamb patties with tomato and oregano salsa
Left Sour-sweet meatballs with red lentils
Below Lamb with eggplant cream and wine sauce

Using hands, combine lamb, paste and lemon grass in large bowl; roll level tablespoons of mixture into balls. Place on tray; cover, refrigerate 30 minutes. *[Can be made ahead to this stage. Cover; refrigerate overnight or freeze.]*

Bring 2 cups (500ml) of the stock to the boil in medium pan; add lentils. Simmer, uncovered, about 10 minutes or until lentils have doubled in size; remove from heat.

Heat oil in large pan; cook meatballs, in batches, until browned all over. Drain on absorbent paper.

Add garlic, onion and ginger to same pan; cook, stirring, until onion is soft. Stir in remaining stock, meatballs, lentil mixture, tomato and pepper. Bring to boil; simmer until meatballs are cooked through and sauce thickens slightly.

SERVES 4

Plate from The Bay Tree Kitchen Shop

LAMB IN A CITRUS MINT SAUCE WITH ROAST VEGIES

2 medium (400g) potatoes
1 medium (400g) kumara
4 medium (300g) egg tomatoes
1/4 cup (60ml) olive oil
1/4 teaspoon sugar
8 lamb loin chops
1 large (200g) onion, sliced
1 clove garlic, crushed
1 tablespoon brown sugar
1 tablespoon balsamic vinegar
1/3 cup (80ml) redcurrant jelly
1/4 cup (60ml) orange juice
1/4 cup (60ml) lemon juice
2 tablespoon chopped fresh
  mint leaves

Cut potatoes, kumara and tomatoes into similar-sized wedges.

Place potato and kumara in single layer in shallow baking dish; brush vegetables with 2 tablespoons of the oil. Bake, uncovered, in hot oven 1 hour.

Place tomato wedges on oven tray, sprinkle with sugar. Bake, uncovered, in hot oven with potato and kumara during the last 15 minutes of cooking time.

Meanwhile, cook lamb in large heated oiled pan, in batches, until browned both sides and cooked as desired. Cover to keep warm.

Heat remaining oil in same pan; cook onion and garlic, stirring, until onion is browned lightly. Add brown sugar; stir until sugar is dissolved. Add remaining ingredients. Bring to boil; simmer, stirring, until jelly melts and sauce thickens slightly. [Sauce can be made ahead. Cover; refrigerate overnight.]

Serve hot citrus mint sauce over lamb, accompanied by roast potato, kumara and tomato wedges.

SERVES 4

COCONUT-CRUMBED CUTLETS AND KUMARA-PARSNIP MASH

1/3 cup finely chopped fresh
  coriander leaves
1/2 cup (25g) flaked coconut
1/2 cup (35g) shredded coconut
1/4 cup (40g) sesame seeds, toasted
12 French-trimmed lamb cutlets
2 tablespoons sesame oil
1 large (500g) kumara,
  chopped coarsely
2 large (360g) parsnips,
  chopped coarsely

Combine coriander, coconuts and seeds large bowl. Brush lamb with oil; coat wi coconut mixture. Cook lamb, in batches, in large heated oiled pan until browned both sides and cooked as desired.

Meanwhile, boil, steam or microwave kumara and parsnips, separately, until tender; drain. Mash together in large bowl; serve with lamb.

SERVES 4 TO 6

Opposite Lamb in a citrus mint sauce with roast vegies
Right Coconut-crumbed cutlets and kumara-parsnip mash

PASTRY-WRAPPED CUTLETS WITH CAPSICUM SALSA

12 lamb cutlets
1 small (150g) red capsicum
1 small (150g) green capsicum
1 small (150g) yellow capsicum
¼ cup (60ml) sweet chilli sauce
1 tablespoon mirin
1 tablespoon peanut oil
1 tablespoon lime juice
1 tablespoon finely chopped fresh coriander leaves
3 sheets ready-rolled puff pastry
1 egg, beaten

Cook cutlets, in batches, in large heated oiled pan until browned both sides.

Halve capsicums, remove and discard seeds and membranes; chop finely. Combine capsicum in medium bowl with sauce, mirin, oil, juice and coriander.

Cut each pastry sheet into 4 triangles. Centre 1 cutlet in each triangle so the bone protrudes from the middle of the longest side of triangle. Place 1 heaped teaspoon of the capsicum salsa on top of each cutlet; fold pastry sides around meaty part of cutlet to form parcel. Trim excess pastry; use to decorate parcel, if desired. *[Can be made ahead to this stage. Cover; refrigerate overnight.]*

Place cutlet parcels on oiled oven tray; brush with egg. Bake, uncovered, in very hot oven about 15 minutes or until pastry is browned and cutlets cooked as desired. Serve with remaining capsicum salsa.

SERVES 4 TO 6

TEX-MEX PIZZA WITH SUNFLOWER SEEDS

We used 3 large (25cm) packaged pizza bases, available from some supermarkets and delicatessens, for this recipe.

2 tablespoons peanut oil
5 cloves garlic, crushed
2 medium (300g) onions, chopped finely
1kg minced lamb
2 teaspoons mustard powder
⅔ cup tomato paste
⅓ cup (80ml) lamb or beef stock
400g can red kidney beans, rinsed, drained
2 tablespoons Cajun seasoning
3 x 335g pizza bases
3 cups (375g) coarsely grated cheddar cheese
1 large (300g) red onion, sliced
⅔ cup (110g) sunflower seed kernels, toasted

Heat oil in medium pan; cook garlic and onion, stirring, until onion is soft. Add lamb; cook, stirring, until browned and cooked through. Stir in mustard powder, paste, stock, beans and half the Cajun seasoning. Bring to boil; simmer, uncovered, 5 minutes or until beans are heated through and mixture thickens slightly. *[Can be made ahead to this stage. Cover; refrigerate overnight or freeze.]*

Place pizza bases on oiled oven trays; spread lamb mixture over bases, top with cheese, onion and extra seasoning. Bake, uncovered, in hot oven about 15 minutes or until pizzas are just browned and bases crisp. Sprinkle with kernels before serving.

SERVES 6 TO 8

RED CURRY, COCONUT AND LAMB STIR-FRY

2 tablespoons peanut oil
500g lamb strips
1 large (200g) onion, sliced
1 tablespoon red curry paste
1 tablespoon finely chopped fresh
** lemon grass**
2 cloves garlic, crushed
1 tablespoon fish sauce
100g snake beans, chopped
600g choy sum, trimmed
1 cup (250ml) coconut cream
1/4 cup finely chopped fresh
** coriander leaves**

Heat half the oil in wok or large pan; stir-fry lamb, in batches, until browned and almost cooked through. Heat remaining oil in pan; stir-fry onion, paste, lemon grass, garlic and sauce until onion is just soft. Add beans and choy sum; stir-fry until vegetables are just tender.

Return lamb to pan with cream and coriander; stir-fry until heated through.

SERVES 4

Opposite above Pastry-wrapped cutlets with capsicum salsa
Opposite Tex-Mex pizza with sunflower seeds
Below Red curry, coconut and lamb stir-fry

CANTONESE LAMB PATTIES

4 Chinese dried mushrooms
1 tablespoon olive oil
1 small (80g) onion, chopped finely
1 tablespoon finely chopped
    lemon grass
2 cloves garlic, crushed
1 tablespoon finely grated
    fresh ginger
1kg minced lamb
3 green onions, chopped

1 tablespoon soy sauce
1 tablespoon hoisin sauce
1/4 teaspoon sesame oil
1 egg, beaten
1/2 cup (35g) breadcrumbs
1 1/2 cups (120g) bean sprouts
1/4 cup (60ml) sweet chilli sauce
1 tablespoon water
1 tablespoon lime juice
1 tablespoon finely chopped fresh
    coriander leaves

Cover mushrooms with boiling water in small heatproof bowl, stand 20 minutes; drain. Remove and discard stems; chop caps finely.

Heat oil in large pan; cook onion, lemon grass, garlic and ginger, stirring, until onion is soft.

Combine mushroom and cooled onion mixture in large bowl with lamb, green onion, sauces, oil, egg and breadcrumbs. *[Can be made ahead to this stage. Cover; refrigerate overnight or freeze.]*

Using hands, shape 1/3 cups of mixture into patties; cook, in batches, in large heated oiled non-stick pan until browned both sides and cooked through.

Serve with sprouts and combined remaining ingredients.

SERVES 4 TO 6

ROSEMARY LAMB SAUSAGES WITH PORT MUSTARD SAUCE

1 medium (200g) red capsicum
800g minced lamb
2 tablespoons tomato paste
2 teaspoons chopped fresh rosemary
4 cloves garlic, crushed
1 teaspoon salt
1 teaspoon cracked black pepper

PORT MUSTARD SAUCE
20g butter
1 small (80g) onion, chopped finely
2 teaspoons plain flour
1 cup (250ml) chicken stock
1/2 cup (125ml) dry red wine
1/4 cup (60ml) port
1 tablespoon Dijon mustard
1 tablespoon tomato paste

Quarter capsicum, remove seeds and membranes. Roast under grill or in very hot oven, skin-side up, until skin blisters and blackens. Cover capsicum pieces in plastic or paper for 5 minutes, peel away skin; chop finely.

Using hands, combine capsicum in large bowl with remaining ingredients; form mixture into 12 sausage shapes. Place on tray; cover, refrigerate 30 minutes. *[Can be made ahead to this stage. Cover; refrigerate overnight or freeze.]*

Cook sausages on heated oiled griddle (or grill or barbecue) until browned all over and cooked through. Serve with Port Mustard Sauce.

Port Mustard Sauce Heat butter in medium pan; cook onion, stirring, about 3 minutes or until soft. Stir in flour; cook over medium heat, stirring, 1 minute. Remove from heat; gradually stir in combined remaining ingredients. Bring to boil; simmer, uncovered, about 15 minutes or until sauce thickens slightly.

SERVES 4 TO 6

TOMATO, BOCCONCINI AND LAMB SALAD

2 lamb mini roasts
2 medium (380g) tomatoes, sliced
1/4 cup firmly packed basil leaves
250g bocconcini cheese, sliced
1/2 cup (125ml) light olive oil
2 tablespoons red wine vinegar
2 teaspoons Dijon mustard
1 teaspoon sugar
1 clove garlic, crushed
2 teaspoons olive paste

Place roasts in large oiled baking dish;
bake, uncovered, in moderate oven about
25 minutes or until cooked as desired.
Cover lamb, stand 5 minutes; slice thinly.
*[Can be made ahead to this stage. Cover;
refrigerate overnight.]*

Layer lamb, tomatoes, basil and
bocconcini on platter; drizzle with
combined remaining ingredients.

SERVES 4

Opposite Cantonese lamb patties
Left Rosemary lamb sausages with
port mustard sauce
Below Tomato, bocconcini and lamb salad

GARLIC-CRUMBED CUTLETS WITH HERBED TOMATO SAUCE

9 slices wholegrain bread
4 cloves garlic, chopped coarsely
3 small fresh red chillies, seeded, chopped coarsely
1/4 cup fresh oregano leaves
2 teaspoons cracked black pepper
12 French-trimmed lamb cutlets
1/4 cup (40g) plain flour
1/3 cup (80ml) milk
2 tablespoons seeded mustard
1 tablespoon olive oil
1 medium (150g) onion, sliced
2 cloves garlic, crushed, extra
400g can tomato pieces
2 tablespoons tomato paste
1/2 cup (125ml) dry white wine
2 tablespoons chopped fresh oregano, extra
1/4 cup (60ml) vegetable oil

Remove and discard crusts from bread; chop bread coarsely. Blend or process bread, chopped garlic, chilli, oregano and pepper just until finely chopped.

Coat lamb in flour; shake off excess. Brush lamb with combined milk and mustard; press on breadcrumb mixture. Cover; refrigerate 30 minutes.

Meanwhile, heat olive oil in medium pan; cook onion and crushed garlic, stirring, about 5 minutes or until onion is browned lightly. Stir in undrained tomatoes, paste, wine and extra oregano; bring to boil. Simmer, uncovered, about 10 minutes or until mixture thickens slightly. *[Can be made ahead to this stage. Cover, separately; refrigerate overnight or freeze.]*

Heat vegetable oil in large pan; cook lamb, in batches, until browned both sides and cooked as desired. Drain; serve with hot tomato sauce.

SERVES 4 TO 6

Plate from The Bay Tree Kitchen Shop

LAMB AND BEAN NACHOS WITH SALSA FRESCA

500g minced lamb
35g packet Taco Seasoning Mix
425g can tomatoes
420g can Mexibeans
1/4 cup (60ml) water
240g plain toasted corn chips
1 cup (125g) coarsely grated cheddar cheese
2 medium (500g) avocados, mashed
1/2 cup (125ml) sour cream

SALSA FRESCA

4 large (360g) egg tomatoes, chopped finely
1 small (100g) red onion, chopped finely
1 tablespoon olive oil
1 tablespoon lemon juice
1 clove garlic, crushed
2 tablespoons finely chopped fresh coriander leaves

Cook lamb in large heated oiled pan, stirring, until browned. Add Seasoning Mix, undrained crushed tomatoes, undrained beans and water; bring to boil. Simmer, uncovered, about 10 minutes or until lamb mixture thickens, stirring occasionally. *[Can be made ahead to this stage. Cover; refrigerate overnight or freeze.]*

Just before serving, spread corn chips over large heatproof plate; top with lamb mixture, sprinkle with cheese. Bake nachos, uncovered, in moderate oven about 15 minutes or until heated through. Combine mashed avocado with half of the Salsa Fresca in a medium bowl; drop spoonfuls of avocado mixture and sour cream over nachos. Top with the remaining Salsa Fresca.

Salsa Fresca Combine all ingredients in medium bowl.

SERVES 4 TO 6

Above Garlic-crumbed cutlets with herbed tomato sauce
Top right Lamb and cashew stir-fry
Right Lamb and bean nachos with salsa fresca

LAMB AND CASHEW STIR-FRY

- 2 tablespoons peanut oil
- 500g lamb strips
- 1 medium (200g) red capsicum, seeded, sliced
- 150g oyster mushrooms
- 500g spinach, trimmed
- 1/4 cup (60ml) oyster sauce
- 2 tablespoons soy sauce
- 3 small dried chillies
- 3 cloves garlic, crushed
- 1 teaspoon grated fresh ginger
- 1 tablespoon brown sugar
- 2 teaspoons cornflour
- 1 tablespoon water
- 2 tablespoons finely shredded fresh basil leaves
- 1 cup (150g) roasted cashews

Heat half the oil in wok or large pan; stir-fry lamb, in batches, until browned all over and almost cooked through. Heat remaining oil in wok; stir-fry capsicum and mushrooms until just tender.

Return lamb to pan with spinach, sauces, whole chillies, garlic, ginger, sugar and blended cornflour and water; stir-fry until sauce boils and thickens. Sprinkle with basil and nuts just before serving.

SERVES 4

LAMB, RED CAPSICUM AND HALOUMI TERRINE

500g lamb eye of loin
1 cup (250ml) boiling water
40g butter
1 cup (200g) couscous
2 eggs, beaten
2 cloves garlic, crushed
2 teaspoons freshly ground
  black pepper
2 large (700g) red capsicums
200g haloumi cheese, sliced
2 tablespoons olive oil
1 tablespoon olive paste

Wrap lamb in plastic wrap; place in freezer about 1 hour or until partially frozen. Discard plastic wrap; slice lamb as thinly as possible. Place, separated, on platter; cover, refrigerate until required.

Combine water and butter in medium heatproof bowl; stir in couscous. Cover; stand about 5 minutes or until water is absorbed. Stir in combined eggs, garlic and pepper.

Quarter capsicums; remove seeds and membranes. Grill capsicum, skin-side up, until skin blisters and blackens. Cover with plastic or paper for 5 minutes, peel away skin. Cut capsicum pieces into wide, even-sized pieces.

Oil two 7cm x 25cm bar pans; line bases and sides with baking paper, extending paper 2cm over opposite sides. Line bases with capsicum, then cheese, then couscous mixture; press down firmly. [Can be made ahead to this stage. Cover; refrigerate overnight.]

Bake, covered, in hot oven about 20 minutes or until terrines are firm. Stand terrines 10 minutes; turn onto board.

Meanwhile, heat 1 tablespoon of the oil in wok or large pan; stir-fry lamb, in batches, until just cooked. Combine remaining oil and olive paste in small bowl. Slice each terrine into 4 pieces; divide among serving plates, top with lamb, drizzle with olive paste mixture.

SERVES 4 TO 6

Plate and napkin from The Bay Tree Kitchen Shop

LAMB, SPINACH AND PECAN SALAD WITH RASPBERRIES

1/3 cup (60g) wild rice
500g lamb fillets
150g baby spinach leaves
1 cup (100g) pecans, toasted
1 small (100g) red onion, sliced
300g frozen raspberries,
  thawed, drained
1/4 cup chopped fresh chives

MAPLE SYRUP DRESSING
1/2 cup (125ml) light olive oil
1 1/2 tablespoons maple syrup
1 tablespoon raspberry vinegar
1 tablespoon seeded mustard
2 teaspoons lemon juice

Cook rice in medium pan of boiling water, uncovered, until tender; drain.

Cook lamb, in batches, on heated oiled griddle (or grill or barbecue) until browned all over and cooked as desired. Cover lamb, stand 5 minutes; slice thickly. [Can be made ahead to this stage. Cover, separately; refrigerate overnight.]

Gently toss rice and lamb in large bowl with remaining ingredients; drizzle over Maple Syrup Dressing.

Maple Syrup Dressing Combine all ingredients in jar; shake well. [Can also be prepared 1 day ahead.]

SERVES 4 TO 6

CHILLI LAMB KEBABS WITH TOMATO BASIL RICE

We used lamb cut from the leg for this recipe. Soak bamboo skewers in water overnight to prevent burning.

1kg diced lamb
1/2 cup (125ml) sweet chilli sauce
2 tablespoons olive oil
2 cloves garlic, crushed
1 tablespoon lime juice
1 teaspoon cracked black pepper

TOMATO BASIL RICE
1 tablespoon olive oil
1 large (200g) onion, chopped
2 cloves garlic, crushed
1 1/2 cups (300g) long-grain white rice
425g can chopped tomatoes
1 1/4 cups (310ml) water
1/2 cup loosely packed basil leaves
2/3 cup (100g) kalamata olives

Combine lamb with remaining ingredients in large bowl, cover; refrigerate 1 hour. *[Can be made ahead to this stage. Cover; refrigerate overnight or freeze.]*

Drain lamb; reserve marinade. Thread lamb onto 12 skewers; cook skewers, in batches, on heated oiled griddle (or grill or barbecue) until browned all over and cooked as desired.

Meanwhile, bring reserved marinade to boil in small pan; simmer, uncovered, 1 minute. Serve lamb with hot marinade and Tomato Basil Rice.

Tomato Basil Rice Heat oil in large pan; cook onion and garlic, stirring, until onion is browned lightly. Add rice, undrained tomatoes and water; bring to boil. Simmer, covered, 12 minutes or until most of the liquid is absorbed. Add basil and olives; stir until just heated through. Remove from heat; stand rice, covered, 10 minutes.

SERVES 4 TO 6

Opposite above Lamb, red capsicum and haloumi terrine
Opposite below Lamb, spinach and pecan salad with raspberries
Left Chilli lamb kebabs with tomato basil rice

GRILLED CHOPS WITH ROAST VEGETABLE ALMOND SAUCE

1 large (350g) red capsicum
1 medium (190g) tomato, halved
4 cloves garlic, unpeeled
2 tablespoons olive oil
1 slice white bread, chopped
1/3 cup (55g) blanched almonds
2 small fresh red chillies, seeded, chopped coarsely
1 teaspoon sweet paprika
2 tablespoons red wine vinegar
1 teaspoon sugar
1/4 cup (60ml) water
1/4 cup (60ml) olive oil, extra
12 lamb forequarter chops

Quarter capsicum, remove seeds and membranes. Place capsicum, tomato and garlic in small oiled baking dish; bake, uncovered, in hot oven about 30 minutes or until capsicum is browned lightly. Cover vegetables for 5 minutes; peel away skins.

Heat oil in medium pan; cook bread and nuts, stirring, about 2 minutes or until browned. Drain on absorbent paper. Add chilli and paprika to same pan; cook, stirring, 1 minute.

Blend or process vegetable mixture, bread mixture, chilli, paprika, vinegar and sugar until smooth. Add water; process until combined. With motor operating, gradually add extra oil; process until combined. [Can be made ahead to this stage. Cover; refrigerate overnight.]

Cook chops on heated oiled griddle (or grill or barbecue) until browned both sides and cooked as desired; serve with sauce.

SERVES 4 TO 6

SICHUAN LAMB AND LEMON SAUSAGES

2 teaspoons Sichuan peppercorns, crushed
3 cloves garlic, crushed
1 teaspoon finely grated fresh ginger
2 tablespoons finely chopped fresh coriander leaves
1 tablespoon finely grated lemon rind
1 tablespoon thick soy sauce
1kg minced lamb

REDCURRANT SAUCE
1 tablespoon olive oil
1 large (300g) red onion, sliced
1 1/4 cups (310ml) beef stock
1 tablespoon finely grated lemon rind
2 tablespoons balsamic vinegar
2 tablespoons Worcestershire sauce
2 tablespoons redcurrant jelly

Using hands, combine sausage ingredients in large bowl; form 1/4 cups of mixture into sausage shapes. Place on tray; cover, refrigerate 30 minutes. *[Can be made ahead to this stage. Cover; refrigerate overnight or freeze.]*

Cook sausages on heated oiled griddle (or grill or barbecue) until browned all over and cooked through. Serve sausages with Redcurrant Sauce.

Redcurrant Sauce Heat oil in medium pan; cook onion, stirring, until soft. Add remaining ingredients; bring to boil, then simmer, uncovered, about 3 minutes or until sauce thickens slightly.

SERVES 4 TO 6

Opposite above Grilled chops with roast vegetable almond sauce
Opposite below Sichuan lamb and lemon sausages
Above Tandoori lamb pizza

TANDOORI LAMB PIZZA

Packaged pizza bases measuring about 25cm across are available from many supermarkets.

500g lamb fillets, sliced finely
1/3 cup (80ml) tandoori paste
200ml yogurt
1 tablespoon olive oil
1 large (200g) onion, sliced
2 cloves garlic, crushed
500g spinach, trimmed
2 tablespoons lemon juice
2 x 335g pizza bases
1 cup (125g) grated pizza cheese
1 teaspoon ground cumin
1 tablespoon water
1/3 cup fresh coriander leaves
1 Lebanese cucumber, chopped
1 large (250g) tomato, chopped
2 tablespoons unsalted roasted peanuts
2 teaspoons olive oil, extra
1 teaspoon lemon juice, extra

Combine lamb with combined paste and half the yogurt in large bowl, cover; refrigerate 3 hours or overnight. *[Can also be frozen, covered, at this stage.]*

Heat oil in large pan; cook lamb, in batches, until browned all over. Drain on absorbent paper. Add onion and garlic to same pan; cook, stirring, until onion is soft. Add spinach and half the lemon juice to pan; cook, stirring, until spinach just wilts.

Place pizza bases on oven trays; sprinkle with cheese, top with spinach mixture and lamb. Bake, uncovered, in hot oven about 15 minutes or until pizzas are just browned and bases crisp.

Meanwhile, whisk cumin and water with remaining juice and yogurt in small bowl; stir in half the coriander.

Sprinkle remaining coriander and combined remaining ingredients over pizzas; serve with yogurt cumin sauce.

SERVES 4 TO 6

Indian setting from Ruby Star Traders

IRISH LAMB CHOP STEW

1 tablespoon olive oil
12 lamb loin chops
2 large (400g) onions, sliced
4 cloves garlic, crushed
425g can crushed tomatoes
2 tablespoons tomato paste
1/2 cup (125ml) dry red wine
1/2 cup (125ml) vegetable stock
1/2 teaspoon ground cinnamon
1/4 teaspoon ground clove
1/4 cup finely chopped fresh parsley
2 large (600g) potatoes
2 medium (240g) carrots, chopped

Heat oil in large pan; cook chops, in batches, until browned both sides. Add onion and garlic to same pan; cook, stirring, until onion is soft. Stir in undrained tomatoes, paste, wine, stock, spices and half the parsley; return lamb to pan. Bring to boil; simmer, covered, 20 minutes.

Meanwhile, halve potatoes; cut each half into 3 wedges. Cut each carrot into 5 pieces. Boil, steam or microwave vegetables, separately, until just tender; drain. Add vegetables to pan; cook, covered, for 10 minutes. *[Can be made ahead to this stage. Cover; refrigerate overnight.]* Serve sprinkled with remaining parsley.

SERVES 4 TO 6

CHILLI, LAMB AND HOKKIEN NOODLE STIR-FRY

750g lamb eye of loin, sliced
2 teaspoons sambal oelek
1 tablespoon fish sauce
1 tablespoon thick soy sauce
2 tablespoons peanut oil
2 cloves garlic, crushed
600g Hokkien noodles
2 tablespoons lime juice
2 tablespoons oyster sauce
2 teaspoons brown sugar
2/3 cup (160ml) beef stock
3/4 cup (50g) shredded coconut, toasted lightly
1/3 cup firmly packed mint leaves, chopped finely
3/4 cup (120g) Brazil nuts, toasted

Combine lamb in large bowl with sambal oelek and both fish and soy sauces; cover, refrigerate 30 minutes. *[Can be made ahead to this stage. Cover; refrigerate overnight or freeze.]*

Drain lamb; reserve marinade. Heat half the oil in wok or large pan; stir-fry lamb and garlic, in batches, until just browned. Cover to keep warm.

Rinse noodles under hot water; drain. Heat remaining oil in same wok; stir-fry noodles, until browned lightly and hot. Remove from wok; cover to keep warm.

Add reserved marinade, juice, oyster sauce, sugar and stock to same wok; bring to boil. Simmer, stirring, about 3 minutes or until sauce thickens slightly. Gently toss lamb, noodles and sauce mixture in large bowl with coconut, mint and nuts.

SERVES 4

Opposite Irish lamb chop stew
Below Chilli, lamb and Hokkien noodle stir-fry

PEPPER STEAKS WITH TOMATO JAM

2 cloves garlic, crushed
2 tablespoons cracked black pepper
2 teaspoons chopped fresh thyme
2 teaspoons finely grated lemon rind
1 tablespoon plain flour
8 lamb steaks
1/4 cup (60ml) olive oil

TOMATO JAM

3 medium (570g) tomatoes, peeled, chopped
1 small (80g) onion, chopped
1 clove garlic, sliced thinly
1 cup (200g) firmly packed brown sugar
2 tablespoons malt vinegar
2 tablespoons lemon juice

Combine garlic, pepper, thyme, rind and flour in a small bowl. Brush lamb with a little of the oil; press pepper mixture onto lamb. *[Can be made ahead to this stage. Cover; refrigerate overnight.]*

Heat remaining oil in large pan; cook lamb, in batches, until browned and cooked as desired. Cover lamb, stand for 5 minutes; serve lamb with Tomato Jam.

Tomato Jam Combine tomato, onion and garlic in medium pan; boil, uncovered, about 3 minutes or until tomatoes are pulpy. Stir in sugar, vinegar and juice; boil, uncovered, about 15 minutes or until mixture becomes thick when tested on a cold saucer. Cool jam before serving. *[Can be made ahead to this stage. Cover; refrigerate up to 3 days.]*

SERVES 4

CHOPS WITH SKORDALIA AND ROASTED CAPSICUM RELISH

Skordalia is a thick Greek sauce made from either mashed potatoes or stale white bread, olive oil and a lot of garlic.

8 lamb chump chops

ROAST CAPSICUM RELISH

6 medium (1.2kg) red capsicums
1 tablespoon olive oil
2 large (400g) onions, sliced
1/4 cup (50g) brown sugar
1/4 cup (60ml) white wine vinegar

SKORDALIA

4 large (1.2kg) potatoes, chopped
1/3 cup (80ml) olive oil
1 tablespoon lemon juice
1 tablespoon white wine vinegar
5 cloves garlic, crushed

Cook chops on heated oiled griddle (or grill or barbecue) until browned both sides and cooked as desired. Serve with Roasted Capsicum Relish and Skordalia.

Roasted Capsicum Relish Quarter capsicums, remove seeds and membranes. Roast under grill or in very hot oven, skin-side up, until skin blisters and blackens. Cover capsicum pieces in plastic or paper for 5 minutes, peel away skin; slice thinly.

Heat oil in large pan; cook onion, stirring, about 5 minutes or until soft. Stir in sugar, vinegar and capsicum; simmer, covered, 10 minutes. Uncover; simmer about 10 minutes or until relish thickens. *[Can be made ahead to this stage. Cover; refrigerate overnight.]*

Skordalia Boil, steam or microwave potato until tender; drain. Place potato in medium pan, mash over low heat; whisk in remaining ingredients until smooth.

SERVES 4

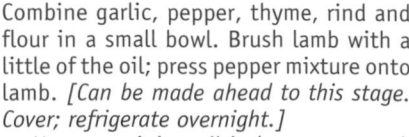

Napkin from The Home Store; spoon from Villeroy & Boch

LAMB SKEWERS ACAPULCO WITH CORN SALSA

Soak bamboo skewers in water several hours or overnight to prevent burning.

600g minced lamb
35g packet Taco Seasoning Mix
1 tablespoon chopped fresh coriander leaves
4 large (23cm) flour tortillas
1 large (320g) avocado
1/4 cup (60ml) sour cream
2 teaspoons lime juice
1 clove garlic, chopped coarsely

CORN SALSA
1 (400g) corn cob
1 medium (190g) tomato, seeded, chopped
1 small (100g) red onion, chopped
2 teaspoons chopped fresh chives
1 tablespoon balsamic vinegar
1 tablespoon olive oil

Using hands, combine lamb with Taco Seasoning and coriander in large bowl; roll level tablespoons of mixture into balls. Thread on 8 skewers, place skewers on tray; cover, refrigerate 30 minutes. *[Can be made ahead to this stage. Cover; refrigerate overnight or freeze.]*

Cut each tortilla into 6 triangles; bake triangles on unoiled oven tray, uncovered, in moderate oven about 15 minutes or until crisp.

Meanwhile, blend or process avocado, sour cream, juice and garlic until smooth. Place in small bowl; cover, refrigerate.

Cook lamb skewers, in batches, on heated oiled griddle (or grill or barbecue) until browned all over and cooked through. Serve skewers with tortilla triangles, creamy avocado and Corn Salsa.

Corn Salsa Remove and discard corn husk and silk; cook corn on heated oiled griddle (or grill or barbecue) until browned lightly all over. Cut kernels from cob; combine with remaining ingredients in small bowl; cover, refrigerate 30 minutes.

SERVES 4

Opposite Pepper steaks with tomato jam
Top right Chops with skordalia and roasted capsicum relish
Right Lamb skewers Acapulco with corn salsa

More than just a roast

◧ You'll be amazed at how many different and imaginative possibilities for a main-course roast you can make by simply alternating your choice of herbs, spices, vegetables and cooking methods. Marinate the meat, or season and roll it, or slow roast it for hours ... there are so many ways to flavour and cook this most succulent of lamb cuts that you'll never have to repeat yourself (but we bet your family will insist that you do).

LAMB WITH LEMONS AND OLIVES

2 medium (280g) lemons
2kg lamb forequarter
1 cup (160g) kalamata olives
10 cloves garlic, unpeeled
¼ cup (60ml) chicken stock
¼ cup (60ml) dry white wine
2 tablespoons finely chopped fresh oregano

Quarter lemons lengthways; place in shallow large baking dish with lamb, olives and garlic. Pour over stock and wine, sprinkle with oregano. *[Can be made ahead to this stage. Cover; refrigerate overnight.]* Bake, uncovered, in moderately slow oven about 2 hours or until cooked as desired.

SERVES 4 TO 6

China and crystal from Waterford Wedgwood; fabric from Boyac Decorative Furnishings

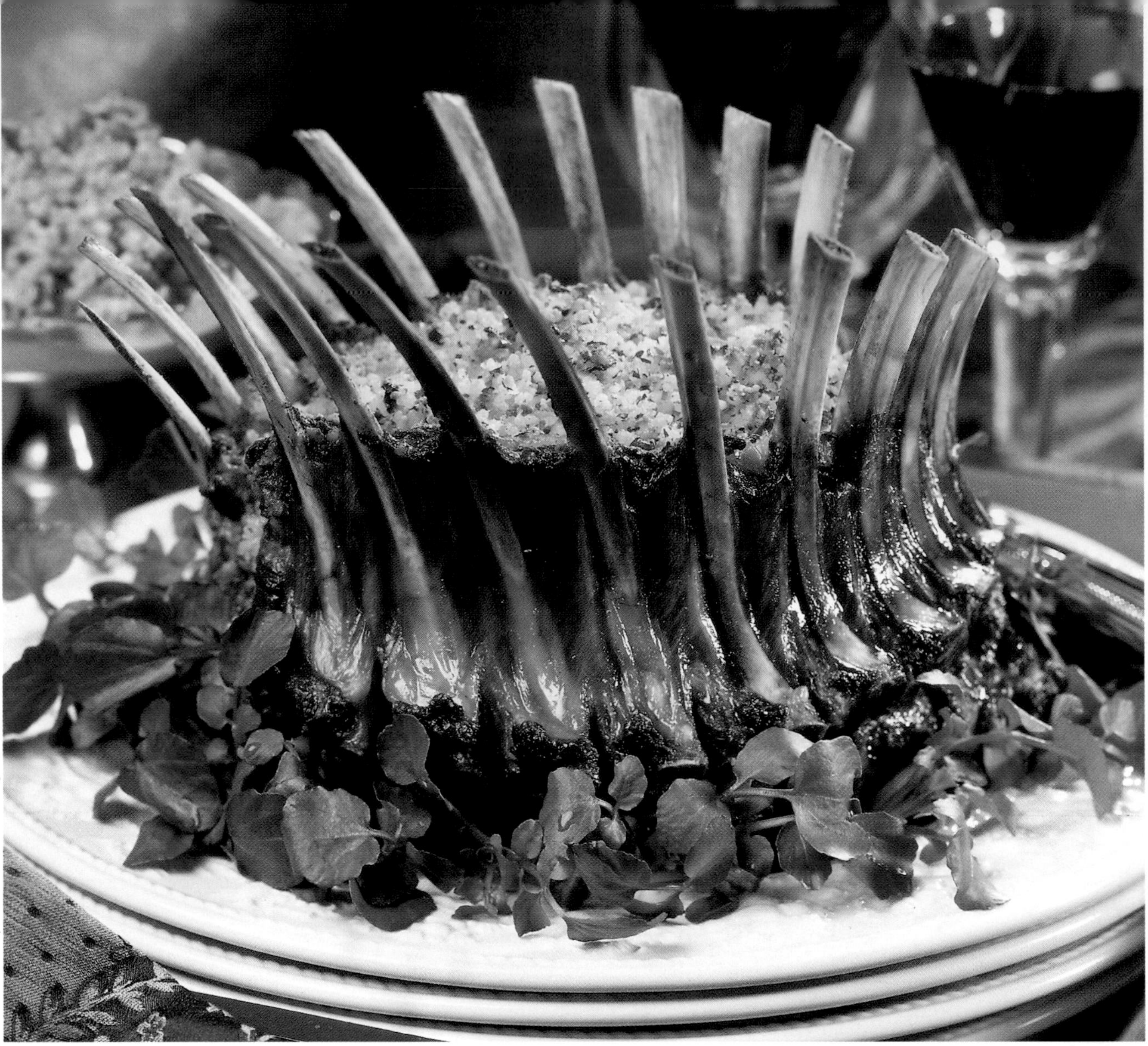

CROWN ROAST WITH HERBED COUSCOUS FILLING

Crown roast of lamb (20 cutlets in 2 separate pieces)
20g butter

COUSCOUS FILLING
2½ cups (625ml) water
80g butter
1¼ cups (250g) couscous
1 large (250g) tomato, seeded, chopped finely
1 small (100g) onion, chopped finely
2 tablespoons finely chopped fresh parsley leaves
2 tablespoons finely chopped fresh coriander leaves
1 teaspoon ground cumin
1 teaspoon cracked black pepper
¼ cup (20g) finely grated parmesan cheese

Remove any skin or fat from lamb bones at top (see picture right). Tie lamb pieces together with kitchen string to resemble a crown. Line large baking dish with foil; place lamb in centre of foil, brush with melted butter, gather foil around exposed bones at base. Place separate pieces of foil around each exposed bone at top (see picture right). *[Can be made ahead to this stage. Cover; refrigerate overnight.]* Bake in hot oven, uncovered, about 20 minutes or until browned lightly. Place Couscous Filling in centre of lamb "crown" (wrap extra filling in foil and place in pan with lamb). Bake in hot oven about 30 minutes or until cooked as desired.

Couscous Filling Bring water to boil in medium pan; stir in butter and couscous. Remove from heat, cover; stand about 5 minutes, fluffing with fork occasionally, until water is absorbed. Gently toss in remaining ingredients.

SERVES 4 TO 6

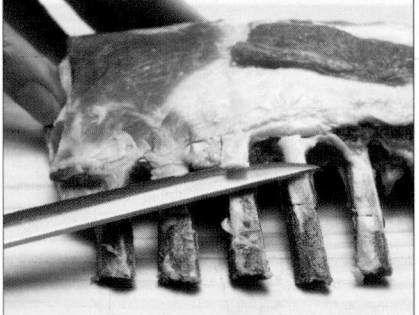

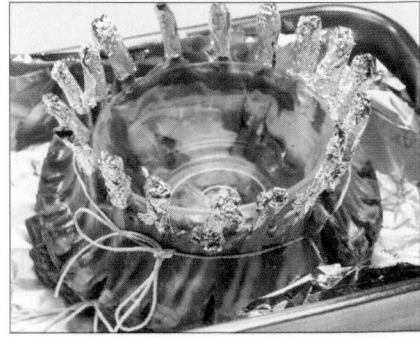

RAAN

This North-Indian take on the Sunday roast will add a note of interest to a family gathering.

2 teaspoons cumin seeds
2 teaspoons coriander seeds
2 teaspoons black mustard seeds
6 cardamom pods, bruised
1/2 teaspoon ground cinnamon
1/2 teaspoon cracked black pepper
1/4 teaspoon ground clove
4 cloves garlic, crushed
1 tablespoon finely grated
   fresh ginger
1/4 cup (60ml) white vinegar
2 tablespoons tomato paste
1 teaspoon sambal oelek
2kg leg of lamb
1/2 cup (125ml) boiling water
4 curry leaves, torn
5 medium (1kg) potatoes, chopped
2 tablespoons ghee
2 teaspoon black mustard
   seeds, extra
2 teaspoons ground cumin
2 teaspoons ground coriander

Combine seeds, pods, cinnamon, pepper and clove in heated large dry pan; cook, stirring, until fragrant. Blend or process cooled spice mixture until crushed; combine in small bowl with garlic, ginger, vinegar, paste and sambal oelek.

Trim lamb; pierce all over with sharp knife. Rub spice mixture all over lamb, pressing firmly into cuts. Place lamb in large bowl; cover, refrigerate overnight. *[Can be made ahead to this stage. Cover; refrigerate up to 2 days or freeze.]*

Pour combined water and curry leaves into large baking dish; place lamb on oven rack in dish. Cover lamb with foil; bake in moderate oven 1 hour. Remove and discard foil; bake about 30 minutes or until lamb is browned and tender.

Meanwhile, boil, steam or microwave potatoes until just tender; drain. Heat ghee in large flameproof baking dish; cook remaining spices, stirring, 1 minute. Add potatoes; cook, stirring, until brown all over. Bake, uncovered, in moderate oven about 15 minutes or until very crisp and well browned; serve with lamb.

SERVES 6 TO 8

Opposite Crown roast with herbed couscous filling
Below Raan, North Indian roast lamb

China from Waterford Wedgwood

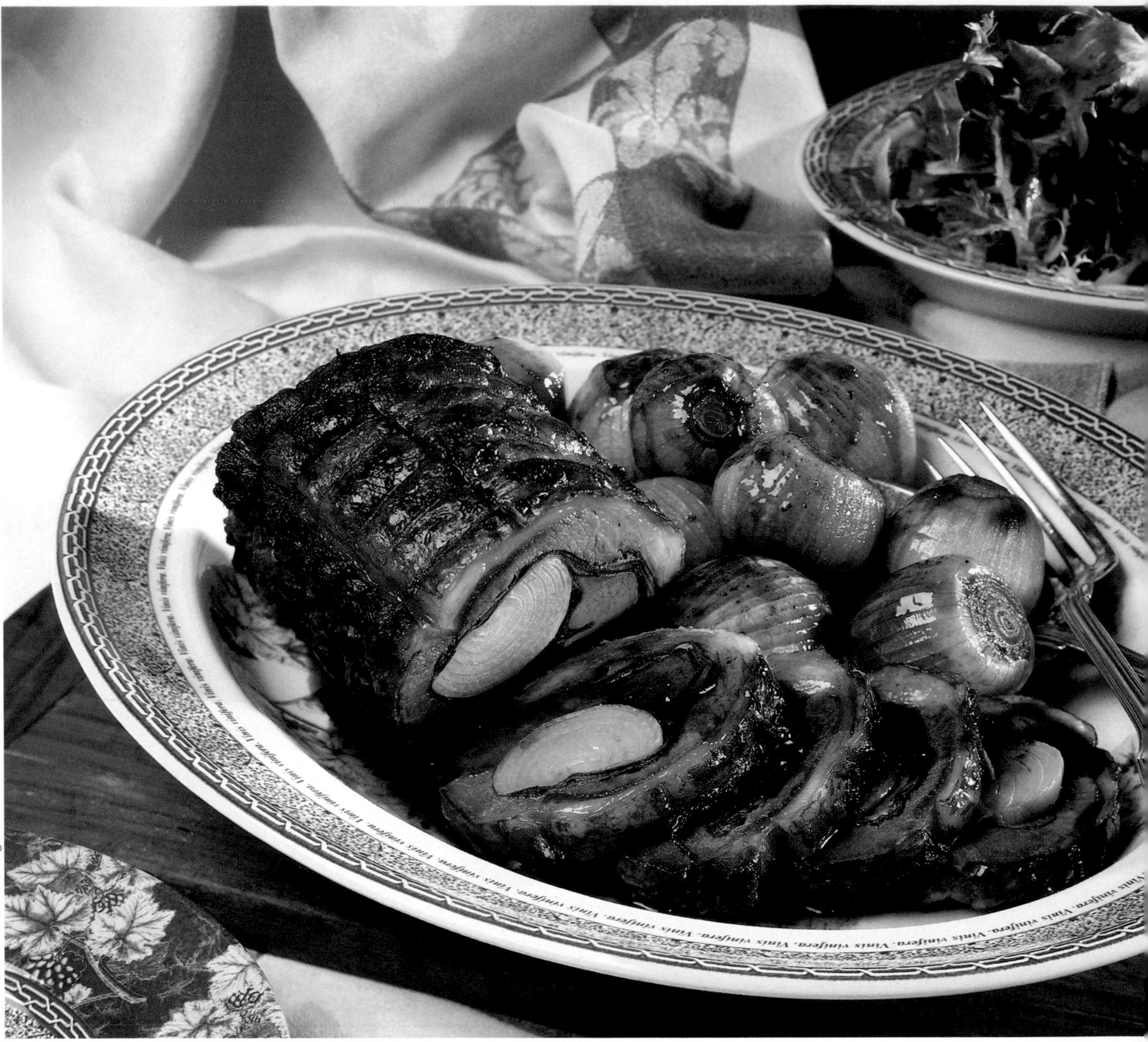

ROLLED ROAST LOIN WITH SPINACH AND PROSCIUTTO

12 (300g) baby onions
1/4 cup (50g) brown sugar
1/4 cup (60ml) balsamic vinegar
1 tablespoon olive oil
650g boned loin of lamb
100g spinach, trimmed
6 slices (90g) prosciutto
1 tablespoon lime juice

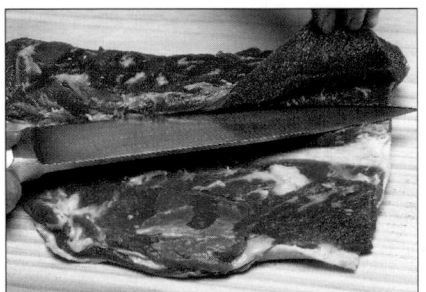

Toss onions in large bowl with combined 2 tablespoons of the sugar, 2 tablespoons of the vinegar and the oil. Place lamb, cut-side up, on board.

Make a horizontal cut through the centre of the meaty eye to create a flap (see above); do not cut all the way through. Lay out flap; place spinach, then prosciutto, over lamb. Halve 2 of the onions crossways; place, in a single row, on prosciutto (see below). Roll lamb over onions, then roll tightly; securing with kitchen string at 2cm intervals. *[Can be made ahead to this stage. Cover; refrigerate overnight.]*

Place lamb and remaining onions in

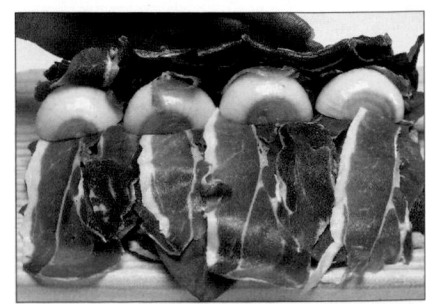

ROAST WITH ROSEMARY AND ANCHOVY BUTTER

2kg leg of lamb
12 (50g) anchovies in oil, drained
3 cloves garlic, sliced finely
2 sprigs fresh rosemary,
**   chopped coarsely**
30g butter, softened
1¾ cups (430ml) dry white wine
¼ cup (60ml) lemon juice

Remove and discard excess fat from lamb. Place lamb in large baking dish, pierce all over with sharp knife; slice 6 anchovies, press anchovy slices, garlic and rosemary into cuts in lamb.

Chop remaining 6 anchovies; combine in small bowl with butter. Rub anchovy butter over lamb, pressing firmly into cuts. Pour combined wine and juice over lamb. *[Can be made ahead to this stage. Cover; refrigerate overnight.]* Bake lamb, uncovered, in moderately hot oven for 15 minutes. Reduce heat to moderate; bake, uncovered, about 1¼ hours or until cooked as desired.

SERVES 6

large oiled flameproof baking dish; brush lamb with some of the vinegar mixture, pour remainder over onions in pan. Bake, uncovered, in hot oven for 15 minutes. Reduce oven to moderate; cover, bake about 45 minutes or until browned and cooked as desired.

Remove lamb and onions from baking dish; cover to keep warm. Skim away fat from pan juices. Add remaining sugar, remaining vinegar and juice to pan juices; bring to boil. Simmer, stirring, about 5 minutes or until sauce reduces slightly. *[Can be made 1 day ahead. Cool, cover; refrigerate overnight.]*

SERVES 4

Above Rolled roast loin with spinach and prosciutto
Right Roast with rosemary and anchovy butter

Platter from The Bay Tree Kitchen Shop; glass and carafe from Stuart Crystal

CYPRIOT LAMB ROAST

2kg leg of lamb
3 cloves garlic, sliced finely
2 teaspoons sprigs fresh thyme
1/2 teaspoon salt
1 teaspoon cracked black pepper
8 small (1kg) potatoes, quartered
2 medium (400g) tomatoes,
    peeled, chopped
2 small (200g) red onions,
    finely sliced
1/2 cup (125ml) dry white wine
2 tablespoons lemon juice
2 tablespoons olive oil
2 bay leaves

Remove and discard excess fat from lamb. Place lamb in large baking dish, pierce all over with sharp knife; press garlic and thyme into cuts in lamb. Sprinkle combined salt and pepper over lamb. *[Can be made ahead to this stage. Cover; refrigerate overnight.]* Bake lamb, uncovered, in moderately slow oven 1 hour. Drain excess fat from pan; place potatoes and tomatoes around lamb, sprinkle with onion. Pour combined remaining ingredients over lamb; bake, uncovered, in moderately slow oven 1 1/2 hours or until lamb is tender. (If lamb starts to overbrown, cover loosely with foil.)

SERVES 6

PISTACHIO-APPLE SEASONED LOIN ROAST

2 tablespoons olive oil
1 small (80g) onion, chopped finely
1 clove garlic, crushed
1 medium (150g) apple, grated
1/4 cup (35g) pistachios,
    toasted, chopped
1 tablespoon finely chopped
    fresh thyme
3/4 cup (50g) stale breadcrumbs
1 egg, beaten
700g boned loin of lamb
1 small (80g) onion, extra
2 tablespoons plain flour
2 cups (500ml) water
1 teaspoon finely chopped fresh
    thyme, extra

Heat half the oil in medium pan; cook chopped onion and garlic, stirring, until onion is soft. Combine onion mixture in large bowl with apple, nuts, thyme, breadcrumbs and egg. *[Can be made ahead to this stage. Cover; refrigerate overnight.]*

Place lamb, cut-side up, on board; cut almost through eye of loin, fold out. Fill with seasoning; roll tightly, secure with kitchen string at 2cm intervals.

Place lamb in large oiled flameproof baking dish with extra whole onion; drizzle with remaining oil. Bake, uncovered, in very hot oven 15 minutes. Reduce heat to moderate; bake, uncovered, about 30 minutes or until cooked as desired.

Transfer lamb to serving dish, cover to keep warm; reserve 2 tablespoons of the pan juices, draining away extra fat. Heat juices, stir in flour; cook, stirring, until mixture is well browned. Remove from heat; gradually stir in water. Bring to boil; simmer, stirring, about 5 minutes or until sauce boils and thickens. Strain over serving bowl; stir in extra thyme.

SERVES 4

Below Cypriot lamb roast
Right Pistachio-apple seasoned loin roast

PORT AND BALSAMIC SLOW-ROASTED LAMB

2.5kg leg of lamb
1/4 cup (40g) sea salt
20g butter
1 tablespoon olive oil
1/3 cup (80ml) dry red wine
1/3 cup (80ml) balsamic vinegar
1/3 cup (80ml) port
1/4 cup (60ml) beef stock
8 cloves garlic, crushed
8 medium (800g) egg tomatoes

Bring a large pan of water to the boil; add lamb, simmer 15 minutes. Drain; pat lamb dry with absorbent paper. Pierce lamb all over with sharp knife; press salt into cuts.

Heat butter and oil in large flameproof baking dish; cook lamb, turning, until browned all over. Pour combined wine, vinegar, port, stock and garlic into baking dish. Bake lamb, covered, in very slow oven for 4 1/2 hours.

Add halved tomatoes, cut-side up; bake further 2 hours, uncovered, basting occasionally. Carefully remove lamb and tomatoes from dish; cover to keep warm. Boil pan juices, stirring, until reduced by half; serve with lamb and tomatoes.

SERVES 6

APRICOT-CURRANT SEASONED GUARD OF HONOUR

30g butter
1 medium (150g) onion, chopped finely
2 cloves garlic, crushed
1/4 cup (35g) dried currants
1/4 cup (35g) dried apricots, sliced finely
1 tablespoon orange juice
1 1/2 cups (105g) stale breadcrumbs
1 tablespoon finely chopped fresh coriander leaves
1 egg, beaten
2 racks of lamb with 6 cutlets each
1/2 teaspoon salt
1/4 teaspoon cracked black pepper
2 teaspoons olive oil
1 clove garlic, crushed, extra
2 tablespoons orange juice, extra

Melt butter in small pan; cook onion and garlic, stirring, until onion is soft. Combine onion mixture in large bowl with currants, apricots, juice, breadcrumbs, coriander and egg. *[Can be made ahead to this stage. Cover; refrigerate overnight.]*

Using sharp knife, tunnel through centre of lamb; fill lamb with seasoning mixture. Interlace racks of lamb (see right), place in large oiled flameproof baking dish. Rub all over lamb with combined salt and pepper; drizzle with oil. Bake, uncovered, in moderate oven about 45 minutes or until browned and cooked as desired.

Transfer lamb to serving dish; cover to keep warm. Heat pan juices, stir in extra garlic and extra juice; simmer, stirring, about 2 minutes or until thick and dark in colour. Serve lamb accompanied by orange glaze.

SERVES 4 TO 6

Plate from Waterford Wedgwood; silver fork from Whitehill Silver

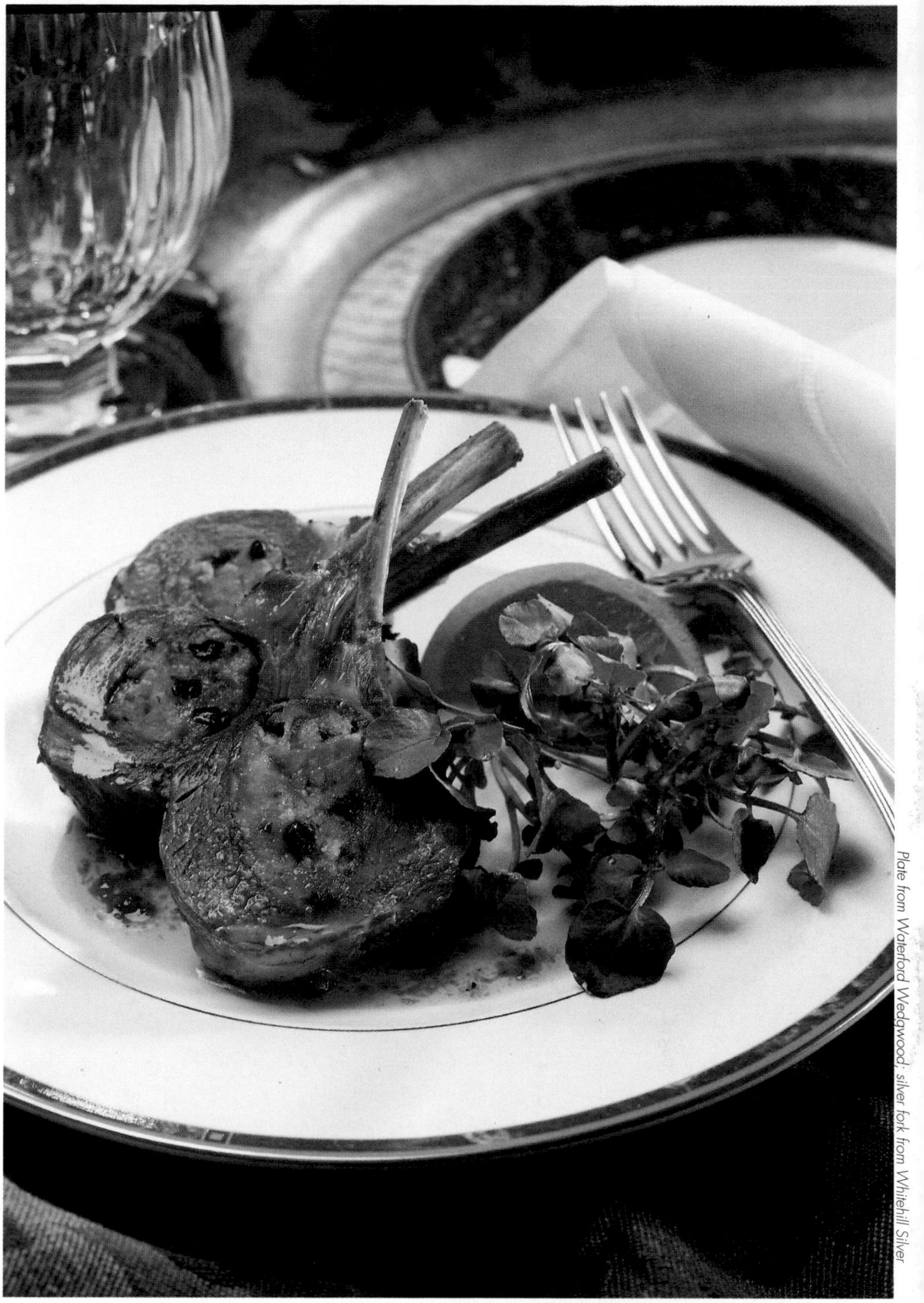

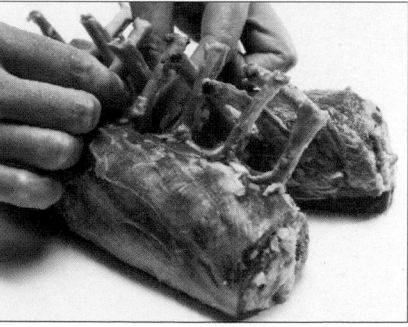

Opposite Port and balsamic slow-roasted lamb
Above Apricot-currant seasoned guard of honour

A roast is so versatile that it can easily assume as many guises as your cooking ingenuity can concoct: flavoured with the best of any season's produce, with those herbs and spices that instantly suggest a particular country's cuisine, or with whatever's to hand in your pantry. The suggestions on the next 6 pages will tastefully start you on your way...

ROAST LEG WITH GARLIC AND ROSEMARY

An average leg of lamb, bone-in, weighs about 2kg and will serve up to 6 people. The suggestions on these 2 pages all use the same size leg, pierced with a sharp knife so the flavours of the seasonings permeate the whole roast.

2kg leg of lamb, trimmed
2 sprigs fresh rosemary, chopped coarsely
8 cloves garlic, sliced finely
20g butter, softened
1 teaspoon cracked black pepper

Pierce lamb all over with sharp knife; place in large baking dish. Press rosemary and garlic firmly into cuts; rub combined butter and pepper over lamb. *[Can be made ahead to this stage. Cover; refrigerate overnight or freeze.]* Bake lamb, uncovered, in moderately hot oven 15 minutes. Reduce heat to moderate; bake, uncovered, about 1¼ hours or until cooked as desired.

SERVES 6

Chermoulla

¼ cup firmly packed fresh
  coriander leaves
¼ cup firmly packed
  flat-leaf parsley
¼ cup (60ml) olive oil
2 tablespoons lemon juice
2 teaspoons ground cumin
1 teaspoon sweet paprika
2 cloves garlic, crushed
2 small fresh red chillies,
  seeded, chopped
½ teaspoon salt

Blend or process all ingredients for the Chermoulla until almost smooth; pour over prepared lamb in baking dish, pressing firmly into cuts. Cover; refrigerate 3 hours or overnight. *[Can be made up to 2 days ahead to this stage. Cover; refrigerate or freeze.]* Cover the lamb loosely with foil; bake in hot oven for 15 minutes. Remove foil, reduce heat to moderate; bake about 1¼ hours or until cooked as desired.

Cajun

1 tablespoon finely chopped
  fresh oregano
2 small fresh red chillies, seeded,
  chopped finely
2 teaspoons sweet paprika
2 teaspoons finely chopped
  fresh thyme
1 teaspoon ground cumin
2 cloves garlic, crushed
50g butter, softened

Combine all ingredients for the Cajun seasoning in small bowl; spread over prepared lamb in baking dish, pressing firmly into cuts. Cover; refrigerate 3 hours or overnight. *[Can be made up to 2 days ahead to this stage. Cover; refrigerate or freeze.]* Cover lamb loosely with foil; bake in hot oven for 15 minutes. Remove foil, reduce heat to moderate; bake for about 1¼ hours or until cooked as desired.

Sun-Dried Tomato and Oregano

2 tablespoons chopped
  sun-dried tomatoes
2 tablespoons sun-dried tomato oil

2 tablespoons coarsely chopped
  fresh oregano
2 tablespoons water
2 tablespoons balsamic vinegar
2 cloves garlic, chopped

Combine all ingredients for the seasoning
in small bowl; spread over prepared lamb
in baking dish, pressing firmly into cuts.
Cover; refrigerate 3 hours or overnight.
*[Can be made up to 2 days ahead to this
stage. Cover; refrigerate or freeze.]* Cover
lamb loosely with foil; bake in hot oven
15 minutes. Remove foil, reduce heat to
moderate; bake about 1¹/4 hours or until
cooked as desired.

Kashmiri

2 teaspoons black mustard seeds
2 teaspoons cumin seeds
1 teaspoon coriander seeds
3 teaspoons garam masala
60g butter, melted

Blend or process seeds until crushed;
combine seeds in small bowl with garam
masala and butter. Spread over prepared
lamb in baking dish, pressing firmly into
cuts. Cover; refrigerate 3 hours or overnight. *[Can be made up to 2 days ahead
to this stage. Cover; refrigerate or freeze.]*
Cover lamb loosely with foil; bake in hot

oven 15 minutes. Remove foil, reduce
heat to moderate; bake about 1¹/4 hours
or until cooked as desired.

Above Roast leg with garlic and rosemary

Redcurrant and Port

2 small (160g) onions
1 tablespoon olive oil
1 clove garlic, crushed
1/4 cup (60ml) redcurrant jelly
1/2 cup (125ml) port
2 tablespoons seeded mustard
**1 tablespoon finely chopped
    fresh rosemary**
1/3 cup (80ml) water

Cut each onion into 8 wedges. Heat oil in small pan; cook onion and garlic, stirring, until onion is browned. Add jelly, port, mustard, rosemary and water; cook, stirring, until jelly melts.

Place lamb, skin-side up, in large shallow baking dish; pour over jelly mixture. Bake, uncovered, in hot oven about 30 minutes or until cooked as desired.

Tandoori

1/2 cup (125ml) tandoori paste
200ml yogurt
2 tablespoons lemon juice
3 cloves garlic, crushed
**1 tablespoon finely chopped fresh
    coriander leaves**
**2 tablespoons finely chopped fresh
    mint leaves**

Combine paste with 1 tablespoon of the yogurt, juice, garlic and coriander in large shallow baking dish; add lamb, coat in marinade. Cover; refrigerate 3 hours or overnight, turning lamb occasionally. *[Can be made up to 2 days ahead to this stage. Cover; refrigerate or freeze.]*

Bake lamb, skin-side up, uncovered, in hot oven about 30 minutes or until cooked as desired. Serve with combined remaining yogurt and mint.

Honey and Chilli

1/2 cup (125ml) honey
1/2 cup (125ml) soy sauce
1/4 cup (60ml) dry sherry
1 tablespoon seeded mustard
3 cloves garlic, crushed
1 tablespoon grated fresh ginger
1 tablespoon sambal oelek

Combine ingredients in large shallow baking dish; add lamb, coat in marinade. Cover; refrigerate 3 hours or overnight, turning lamb occasionally. *[Can be made up to 2 days ahead to this stage. Cover; refrigerate or freeze.]*

Bake lamb, skin-side up, uncovered, in hot oven about 30 minutes or until cooked as desired.

ROAST BUTTERFLIED LEG WITH ORANGE AND MADEIRA

Ask your butcher to butterfly a 2kg leg for you, or do it yourself, by cutting along the line of the bone and removing it. Butterflying a leg decreases cooking time dramatically.

1/2 cup (125ml) orange juice
1/2 cup (125ml) orange marmalade
1/4 cup (60ml) Madeira
2 teaspoons sweet paprika
3 cloves garlic, crushed
1.5kg butterflied leg of lamb
1 medium (180g) orange

Pour the combined juice, marmalade, Madeira, paprika and garlic over lamb in a large shallow baking dish. Cover; refrigerate 3 hours or overnight, turning lamb occasionally so marinade coats all sides. *[Can be made up to 2 days ahead to this stage. Cover; refrigerate or freeze.]*

Cut orange into 8 wedges; place in dish with lamb. Bake lamb, skin-side up, uncovered, in hot oven about 30 minutes or until cooked as desired.

SERVES 4 TO 6

Platter and spoon from The Home Store

ROAST SHOULDER ITALIAN-STYLE

An average lamb shoulder, bone-in, trimmed weighs around 1.7kg and serves 4 to 6. The other seasoning suggestions on this page all use the same weight cut of lamb.

1.7kg lamb shoulder
6 garlic cloves, peeled
6 sprigs fresh oregano
2 tablespoons olive oil
6 baby (150g) onions, halved
2 cloves garlic, crushed, extra
4 baby (240g) eggplant
4 small (360g) zucchini
4 small (240g) egg tomatoes
2 tablespoons balsamic vinegar
1 tablespoon olive oil, extra

Pierce fattest part of lamb in 6 places with sharp knife; press garlic and oregano into cuts. *[Can be made ahead to this stage. Cover; refrigerate overnight or freeze.]*

Heat oil in large flameproof baking dish; cook onion and the extra garlic, stirring, until the onion is browned. Halve the eggplant and zucchini lengthways; quarter tomatoes.

Centre lamb in baking dish; surround with vegetables, brush with combined vinegar and extra oil. Bake, covered, in moderate oven for 1 hour. Drain off pan juices; bake, uncovered, about 45 minutes or until cooked as desired.

SERVES 4 TO 6

Apricot and Almond

2 tablespoons blanched almonds
9 (50g) dried apricots
9 whole cloves
1/4 cup (60ml) apricot jam
1/4 cup (60ml) sweet fruit chutney
2 tablespoons port

Pierce fattest part of lamb in 6 places with sharp knife; press almonds into cuts. Secure apricots to lamb with cloves. *[Can be made ahead to this stage. Cover; refrigerate overnight or freeze.]*

Place lamb in large baking dish. Heat combined jam, chutney and port in small pan, stirring, until jam melts. Brush half the jam chutney mixture over lamb; bake, covered, in moderate oven 1 hour. Uncover; bake about 45 minutes or until cooked as desired, brushing occasionally with remaining apricot mixture.

Opposite Roast butterflied leg with orange and Madeira
Right Roast shoulder Italian-style

Mixed-Grain and Pepper Crust

8 slices multi-grain bread
2 cloves garlic, halved
1 tablespoon cracked black pepper
1 tablespoon chopped fresh basil leaves
2 teaspoons chopped fresh oregano
1/3 cup (80ml) olive oil

Blend or process all ingredients until well combined; press over lamb in large baking dish. *[Can be made ahead to this stage. Cover; refrigerate overnight or freeze.]*

Bake lamb, covered, in moderate oven 1 hour; uncover, bake about 45 minutes or until cooked as desired.

Browned Potato Crust

1/4 cup (60ml) olive oil
2 cloves garlic, crushed
1 teaspoon cracked black pepper
4 medium (800g) potatoes, chopped
2 tablespoons milk
20g butter
1/3 cup (25g) coarsely grated parmesan cheese
2 teaspoons finely chopped fresh rosemary

Pour combined oil, garlic and pepper over the lamb in large baking dish. Cover; refrigerate 3 hours or overnight, turning lamb occasionally to coat with seasoned oil. *[Can be made up to 2 days ahead to this stage. Cover; refrigerate or freeze.]*

Boil, steam or microwave potatoes until very tender; drain. Push potatoes through coarse sieve into large bowl; stir in milk, butter, cheese and rosemary.

Bake lamb, covered, in moderate oven 1 hour. Spread potato mixture over lamb; bake, uncovered, about 45 minutes or until cooked as desired.

Chilli and Lime

2 teaspoons chilli powder
1 tablespoon finely grated lime rind
2 tablespoons lime juice
1/3 cup (80ml) coconut milk
1 teaspoon cracked black pepper

Pour combined ingredients over lamb in large baking dish. Cover, refrigerate 3 hours or overnight, turning lamb occasionally. *[Can be made up to 2 days ahead to this stage. Cover; refrigerate or freeze.]*

Bake lamb, covered, in moderate oven 1 hour. Bake, uncovered, for about 45 minutes or until cooked as desired.

Baking dish from le Creuset

TUNNEL-BONED LAMB WITH CORIANDER HAZELNUT PESTO

The following of seasonings are sufficient for either a 2kg leg of lamb, tunnel-boned, or a 1.7kg lamb shoulder, tunnel-boned.

1/3 cup (50g) unroasted hazelnuts
1/2 cup firmly packed fresh coriander leaves
1/3 cup firmly packed fresh basil leaves
1 tablespoon finely grated fresh ginger
5 cloves garlic, crushed
2 tablespoons lime juice
2 teaspoons fish sauce
1 teaspoon brown sugar
2 tablespoons olive oil
2kg leg of lamb, tunnel-boned, OR 1.7kg lamb shoulder, tunnel-boned

Spread nuts in single layer on oven tray; toast, uncovered, in moderately hot oven about 5 minutes or until skins begin to flake. Rub hazelnuts in soft cloth to remove skins; cool.

Blend or process nuts, leaves, ginger, garlic, juice, sauce and sugar until pureed. With motor operating, gradually pour in oil; process until pesto thickens. *[Can be made ahead to this stage. Cover; refrigerate overnight or freeze.]*

Spread half the pesto inside boned cavity of lamb; spread half the remaining pesto along centre of lamb. Roll from short side to enclose pesto; secure lamb with skewers, tie with kitchen string at 2cm intervals. Place lamb on wire rack in large baking dish. Press remaining pesto onto outside of lamb.

Bake, uncovered, in moderate oven about 1 3/4 hours or until cooked as desired. Cover lamb loosely with foil; stand 20 minutes before carving.

SERVES 6 TO 8

Cheddar and Potato Mash

4 small (480g) potatoes, quartered
1/4 cup (60ml) olive oil
2 cloves garlic, crushed
1 small (200g) leek, sliced
4 slices (45g) pancetta, chopped
1/2 cup (60g) coarsely grated matured cheddar cheese
1/4 cup (40g) chopped raisins

Boil, steam or microwave potatoes until tender; drain. Place potato in small bowl; mash until smooth.

Heat 1 tablespoon of the oil in medium pan; cook garlic and leek, stirring, until soft. Remove from heat, stir in potato, pancetta, cheese and raisins. *[Can be made ahead to this stage. Cover; refrigerate overnight or freeze.]*

Spread a quarter of the potato seasoning inside boned cavity of lamb; spread another quarter of the seasoning along centre of lamb. Roll from short side to enclose seasoning; secure lamb with skewers, tie with kitchen string at 2cm intervals. Shape any remaining seasoning into a log; wrap in oiled foil, twist ends to secure. Place lamb on wire rack in large baking dish, brush with remaining oil.

Bake, uncovered, in moderate oven 1 hour. Place seasoning log on wire rack with lamb; cook lamb, uncovered, another 30 minutes. Cover lamb loosely with foil; stand 20 minutes before carving.

Roasted Capsicum and Broad Beans

1 small (150g) red capsicum
3/4 cup (150g) long-grain white rice
1 1/2 cups (325ml) water
1/2 teaspoon salt
100g frozen broad beans, cooked, peeled
1/2 cup (40g) flaked almonds, toasted
2 tablespoons roughly chopped fresh coriander leaves
3 teaspoons sumac
2 tablespoons olive oil

Quarter capsicum, remove seeds and membranes. Roast under grill or in very hot oven, skin-side up, until skin blisters and blackens. Cover capsicum in plastic or paper for 5 minutes, peel away skin; slice capsicums into 1cm pieces.

Bring rice, water and salt to boil in medium pan; simmer, covered, for about 10 minutes or until rice is tender. Remove from heat. Toss capsicum and rice in large bowl with beans, almonds, coriander and sumac. *[Can be made ahead to this stage. Cover; refrigerate overnight or freeze.]*

Spread a quarter of vegetable-rice seasoning inside boned cavity of lamb; spread another quarter seasoning down centre of lamb. Roll from short side to enclose seasoning; secure lamb with skewers, tie with kitchen string at 2cm intervals. Shape any remaining seasoning into a log; wrap in oiled foil, twist ends to secure. Place lamb on wire rack in large baking dish, brush with oil.

Bake, uncovered, in moderate oven 1 hour. Place seasoning log on wire rack with lamb; cook lamb, uncovered, for another 30 minutes. Cover lamb loosely with foil; stand 20 minutes before carving.

Couscous, Rocket and Dried Fruits

3/4 cup (165g) couscous
3/4 cup (180ml) vegetable stock
3/4 cup (130g) pine nuts, toasted, chopped
3/4 cup shredded rocket
1/2 cup (75g) dried currants
1/3 cup (55g) dried dates, seeded, chopped
1 egg, lightly beaten
2 tablespoons olive oil

Place couscous in large bowl; stir in hot stock; stand 4 minutes or until all liquid is absorbed. Fluff couscous with fork; gently stir in nuts, rocket, fruit and egg in same bowl. *[Can be made ahead to this stage. Cover; refrigerate overnight.]*

Place about a quarter of the couscous seasoning inside boned cavity of lamb; place another quarter seasoning down centre of lamb. Roll from short side to enclose seasoning; secure lamb with skewers, tie with kitchen string at 2cm intervals. Shape any remaining seasoning into a log; wrap in oiled foil, twist ends to secure. Place lamb on wire rack in large baking dish, brush with remaining oil.

Bake, uncovered, in moderate oven

1 hour. Place seasoning log on wire rack with lamb; cook lamb, uncovered, another 30 minutes. Cover lamb loosely with foil; stand 20 minutes before carving.

Figs and Buttered Walnuts

1/4 cup (45g) wild rice
3/4 cup (180ml) water
1/3 cup (50g) cracked wheat
20g butter
1 teaspoon fennel seeds
1/4 teaspoon ground cinnamon
1/3 cup (85g) chopped glace figs
1/2 cup (60g) chopped walnuts
1 tablespoon lemon juice
1 tablespoon honey

Bring rice and water to boil in small pan; simmer, covered, for about 20 minutes or until tender. Remove from heat.

Meanwhile, cover wheat with cold water in medium pan; bring to boil. Simmer, uncovered, about 15 minutes or until just tender; drain. Heat butter in medium pan; cook seeds, cinnamon, figs and nuts, stirring, about 4 minutes or until nuts are browned lightly. Combine nut mixture in large bowl with rice and wheat. *[Can be made ahead to this stage.*

Cover; refrigerate overnight or freeze.]

Spread half of the fig seasoning inside boned cavity of lamb; spread remaining seasoning down centre of lamb. Roll from short side to enclose seasoning; secure lamb with skewers, tie with kitchen string at 2cm intervals. Place lamb on wire rack in large baking dish; brush with combined juice and honey.

Bake, uncovered, in moderate oven about 1 3/4 hours or until cooked as desired. Cover lamb loosely with foil; stand 20 minutes before carving.

Buckwheat Noodles and Lime

10 (20g) Chinese dried mushrooms
70g buckwheat noodles (soba)
1/3 cup (50g) toasted peanuts, chopped
2 tablespoons chopped fresh coriander leaves
2 kaffir lime leaves, sliced
2 teaspoons fresh ginger, grated
3 cloves garlic, crushed
1 small fresh red chilli, chopped
2 teaspoons tamarind concentrate
2 tablespoons lime juice
2 tablespoons palm sugar
2 tablespoons peanut oil

Place mushrooms in heatproof bowl, cover with boiling water; stand 20 minutes. Drain mushrooms; discard the stems, chop caps finely.

Cook noodles in large pan of boiling water, uncovered, until just tender; drain. Rinse well under cold water; drain again, chop roughly.

Blend or process nuts, leaves, ginger, garlic, chilli, tamarind, juice and sugar until pureed. Combine nut mixture in large bowl with mushrooms and noodles.

Spread half the noodle seasoning inside boned cavity of lamb; spread remaining half seasoning along centre of lamb. Roll from short side to enclose seasoning; secure lamb with skewers, tie with kitchen string at 2cm intervals. Place lamb on wire rack in large baking dish; brush with oil.

Bake, uncovered, in moderate oven about 1 3/4 hours or until cooked as desired. Cover lamb loosely with foil; stand 20 minutes before carving.

Below Tunnel-boned lamb with coriander hazelnut pesto

Traditional favourites

Lamb is eaten by almost every culture, and we've adopted many of the world's classic dishes as our own: today, we are about as familiar with moussaka, kofta and Mongolian garlic lamb as we are with a chop or roast, but there remains a wealth of delectable discoveries to be made — and these exciting examples are certain to whet your appetite for more.

MONGOLIAN GARLIC LAMB

1kg lamb strips
1 teaspoon five-spice powder
2 teaspoons sugar
3 cloves garlic, crushed
1 egg, beaten
1 tablespoon cornflour
1¹/₂ tablespoons rice wine vinegar
¹/₃ cup (80ml) soy sauce
1 tablespoon black bean sauce
¹/₄ cup (60ml) peanut oil
3 medium (450g) onions, sliced thinly
¹/₃ cup (80ml) beef stock
¹/₄ teaspoon sesame oil
2 green onions, sliced finely

Combine lamb in large bowl with the five-spice, sugar, garlic and egg. Blend cornflour with vinegar and half the sauces; stir into lamb mixture. Cover; refrigerate 1 hour. *[Can be made ahead to this stage. Cover; refrigerate overnight.]*

Drain lamb over small bowl; reserve the marinade. Heat half the peanut oil in wok or large pan; stir-fry lamb, in batches, until browned and almost cooked through. Heat remaining peanut oil in wok; stir-fry onions until soft. Return lamb to wok with the reserved marinade, remaining sauces, stock and sesame oil; cook, stirring, until mixture boils and thickens. Serve sprinkled with green onion.

SERVES 4 TO 6

Soup tureen from House In Newtown

SPICED SAMOSAS WITH COCONUT RAISIN RAITA

Pomegranate powder is available from Indian, Middle-Eastern or health food stores. We used trimmed and minced lamb shoulder in this recipe.

1 tablespoon vegetable oil
2 cloves garlic, crushed
1 medium (150g) onion, chopped finely
1 medium (200g) potato, chopped finely
300g minced lamb
1/2 teaspoon ground cardamom
1/2 teaspoon ground cinnamon
1 teaspoon pomegranate powder
1 tablespoon tomato paste
1/4 cup (60ml) lamb or beef stock
2 tablespoons finely chopped fresh coriander leaves
4 sheets ready-rolled puff pastry
1 egg, beaten

COCONUT RAISIN RAITA
1 cup (160g) raisins, chopped
1/2 cup (45g) desiccated coconut, toasted
400ml yogurt
1 tablespoon lime juice

Heat oil in medium pan; cook garlic, onion and potato until onion is soft. Add lamb; cook, stirring, until lamb is browned and cooked through. Add spices, paste and stock, bring to boil; simmer, stirring, about 5 minutes or until potato is tender. Remove from heat, stir in coriander leaves; cool. *[Can be made ahead to this stage. Cover; refrigerate overnight or freeze.]*

Cut 8cm rounds from pastry sheets (you should get 9 rounds from each sheet). Centre 1 level tablespoon of filling on each round; fold over and press edges together to seal. Place samosas 3cm apart on oiled oven trays. *[Can be made 3 hours ahead to this stage. Cover tightly with plastic wrap; refrigerate.]*

Brush samosas with egg; bake, uncovered, in moderate oven about 35 minutes or until browned and crisp. Serve immediately, accompanied by Coconut Raisin Raita.

Coconut Raisin Raita Combine all raita ingredients in a small bowl. Cover; refrigerate for 1 hour before serving.

MAKES 36

CURRIED MUTTON SOUP

The diced mutton will have to be ordered in advance from your butcher.

4 small fresh red chillies, halved, seeded
3cm piece fresh ginger, chopped coarsely
1 cup loosely packed fresh mint leaves
1 teaspoon ground fennel
1 teaspoon ground cumin
1 teaspoon ground cardamom
2 teaspoons curry powder
2 tablespoons vegetable oil
600g diced mutton

1.5 litres (6 cups) lamb or beef stock
2 medium (400g) tomatoes, chopped finely
1/2 cup (100g) long-grain white rice

Blend or process the chilli, ginger, mint, spices and curry powder until smooth.

Heat oil in large pan; cook mutton, in batches, until browned all over. Return mutton to pan with spice mixture, stock and tomatoes. Bring to boil; simmer, covered, about 1 hour or until mutton is tender. *[Can be made ahead to this stage. Cover; refrigerate overnight.]* Add rinsed rice, bring to boil; simmer, covered, about 20 minutes or until rice is just tender.

SERVES 4

Left Curried mutton soup
Top right Spiced samosas with coconut raisin raita
Right Lamb shank and vegetable soup

Tray from Ruby Star Traders

LAMB SHANK AND VEGETABLE SOUP

1 tablespoon olive oil
6 lamb shanks
4 bacon rashers
1 medium (150g) onion, chopped
2 cloves garlic, crushed
2 sticks (150g) trimmed celery,
   sliced thinly
1 bunch (400g) baby carrots
4 small (280g) turnips, halved
150g small Swiss brown mushrooms
$1/2$ cup (100g) yellow split peas
400g can tomatoes
$1/4$ cup (60ml) tomato paste
$1/4$ cup (60ml) dry red wine
2.5 litres (10 cups) vegetable stock
2 dried bay leaves
1 cup (150g) frozen broad beans,
   thawed, peeled

Heat oil in large pan; cook lamb, in batches, until browned all sides.

Remove and discard rind from bacon; chop bacon finely. Place bacon, onion and garlic in same pan; cook, stirring, until onions are browned lightly. Add celery, carrots, turnips and whole mushrooms; cook, stirring, until vegetables are just soft.

Return lamb to pan; add split peas, undrained crushed tomatoes, paste, wine, vegetable stock and bay leaves. Bring to boil; simmer, covered, about $1^{1}/_2$ hours or until lamb is tender. Cover; refrigerate overnight. *[Must be made 1 day ahead. Can also be refrigerated, covered, for up to 2 days or frozen at this stage.]*

Remove all fat solids from surface of soup before reheating. Add broad beans; cook, stirring, until heated through.

SERVES 4 TO 6

Bowls from Orson & Blake Collectables

TURKISH PIZZA

1½ teaspoons dried yeast
1¼ cups (310ml) warm water
1 teaspoon sugar
1½ teaspoons salt
3 cups (450g) plain flour
2 tablespoons olive oil

ONION TOPPING
2 tablespoons olive oil
2 large (400g) onions, sliced
2 cloves garlic, crushed

LAMB TOPPING
1 tablespoon olive oil
2 cloves garlic, crushed
600g minced lamb
½ teaspoon ground cinnamon
2½ teaspoons mixed spice
½ cup (80g) pine nuts,
  toasted, chopped
1 tablespoon lemon juice

HERB TOPPING
¼ cup finely chopped fresh parsley
¼ cup finely chopped fresh
  mint leaves
2 medium (260g) tomatoes, peeled,
  seeded, chopped

YOGURT TOPPING
½ cup (125ml) yogurt
¼ cup (60ml) water

Whisk yeast, water, sugar and salt together in small bowl; cover, stand in warm place about 10 minutes or until mixture is frothy.

Sift flour into large bowl, stir in yeast mixture and oil; mix to a soft dough. Knead dough on floured surface about 5 minutes or until smooth. Place dough in oiled large bowl, cover; stand in warm place about 40 minutes or until doubled in size.

Halve dough; knead each half for 5 minutes. Place each half in separate oiled medium bowls, cover; stand in warm place about 30 minutes or until doubled in size.

Roll each portion of dough into an oval measuring approximately 18cm x 40cm; place each oval-shaped pizza base on separate oiled oven tray. Divide Onion Topping and Lamb Topping between the 2 bases, leaving 5cm border. Bake, uncovered, in very hot oven for about 25 minutes or until bases are cooked through and tops browned. Sprinkle pizzas with Herb Topping; drizzle with Yogurt Topping.

Onion Topping Heat oil in large pan; cook onion and garlic, stirring, until onion is soft and browned. Cool.

Lamb Topping Heat oil in large pan; cook garlic, stirring, 1 minute. Add lamb; cook, stirring, until browned through. Stir in cinnamon, mixed spice, nuts and juice.

Herb Topping Combine all ingredients in small bowl.

Yogurt Topping Whisk yogurt and water together in small jug.

Onion, Lamb and Yogurt Toppings can be made ahead. Cover, separately; refrigerate overnight. Herb Topping best made while pizzas bake.

SERVES 4 TO 6

Left Turkish pizza
Right Mexican black bean soup with lamb

MEXICAN BLACK BEAN SOUP WITH LAMB

2 cups (400g) dried black beans
2.5 litres (10 cups) water
400g whole piece boneless lamb
    shoulder, halved
1 small (200g) leek, chopped finely
1 small (70g) carrot, chopped finely
1½ cups (375ml) lamb or beef stock
1 tablespoon olive oil
3 cloves garlic, crushed
1 small (100g) red onion,
    chopped finely
1 small (150g) red capsicum,
    chopped finely
2 teaspoons ground cumin
1 cup (250ml) lime juice
⅓ cup (80ml) dry sherry
¼ cup (60ml) balsamic vinegar
1 medium (190g) tomato,
    seeded, chopped
1 tablespoon salt

ACCOMPANIMENTS
½ cup finely chopped fresh
    coriander leaves
1 large (300g) red onion, chopped
½ cup (125ml) sour cream
8 small fresh red chillies,
    seeded, chopped
¼ cup (60ml) white wine vinegar
2 limes

Cover beans with cold water in large bowl; stand overnight.

Drain the beans then rinse under cold water; drain. Bring 2 litres of the water to boil in large pan. Add lamb; simmer, covered, about 1½ hours or until tender. Drain lamb over medium bowl; reserve liquid. Place cooled lamb in separate large bowl; using fork, shred finely.

Return reserved lamb cooking liquid to same pan with beans, leek, carrot, stock and remaining 2 cups water. Bring to boil; simmer, uncovered, about 1 hour or until beans are tender. Remove from heat.

Heat oil in small pan; cook garlic, onion, capsicum and cumin, stirring, until onion is soft. Add to bean mixture with juice, sherry, vinegar, tomato, salt and shredded lamb.

Blend or process half the bean soup, in batches, until almost smooth; return to same pan with remaining soup. *[Can be made ahead to this stage. Cover; refrigerate overnight.]* Reheat; when heated through, serve with separate bowls of various accompaniments.

Accompaniments Combine coriander, onion and cream in a small bowl. Combine chilli and vinegar in another small bowl. Place lime wedges in third small bowl.

SERVES 6 TO 8

PASTITSIO

This Greek dish of macaroni and lamb baked with bechamel sauce is not as well-known among non-Greeks as is moussaka, but it's so tasty it's sure to become a family favourite.

**250g ziti (or any long,
   thick macaroni)**
20g butter, melted
2 eggs, beaten
1/2 teaspoon ground nutmeg
**1 cup (80g) grated pecorino or
   romano cheese**

MEAT SAUCE
2 tablespoons olive oil
**1 large (200g) onion,
   chopped finely**
2 cloves garlic, crushed
750g minced lamb
400g can tomatoes
1/2 cup (125ml) lamb or beef stock
1/4 cup (60ml) dry red wine
1/4 cup (60ml) tomato paste
1/2 teaspoon ground cinnamon
1 tablespoon chopped fresh parsley
1 egg, beaten

BECHAMEL SAUCE
90g butter
1/2 cup (70g) plain flour
3 cups (750ml) milk
**1/2 cup (40g) grated pecorino or
   romano cheese**
1/4 teaspoon ground nutmeg
2 egg yolks, beaten

Cook ziti in large pan of boiling water, uncovered, until just tender; drain. Combine cooled ziti in large bowl with butter and eggs combined with nutmeg and three-quarters of the cheese. Spread ziti mixture over base of oiled deep 3-litre (12-cup) ovenproof dish. Top with Meat Sauce; pour over the Bechamel Sauce, sprinkle with remaining cheese. *[Can be made ahead to this stage. Cover; refrigerate overnight.]* Bake, uncovered, in moderate oven about 45 minutes or until browned and cooked through.

Meat Sauce Heat oil in pan; cook onion and garlic, stirring, until onion is soft. Add lamb; cook, stirring, until lamb is cooked through. Stir in undrained crushed tomatoes, stock, wine, paste, cinnamon and parsley. Bring to boil; simmer, uncovered, about 30 minutes or until sauce thickens. Stir in egg. *[Can be made ahead. Cover; refrigerate overnight or freeze.]*

Bechamel Sauce Heat butter in large pan; cook flour, stirring, about 1 minute or until bubbling. Remove from heat; gradually stir in milk. Return to heat; cook, stirring, until sauce boils and thickens. Cool slightly; stir in combined cheese, nutmeg and egg yolks.

SERVES 6 TO 8

EMPANADAS WITH SALSA ROJA AND SPICED PEPITAS

**1kg whole piece boneless lamb
   shoulder, halved**
2 tablespoons peanut oil
5 cloves garlic, crushed
2 tablespoons sugar
3 teaspoons ground allspice
2 teaspoons ground cinnamon
1/3 cup (80ml) lime juice
1/2 cup (125ml) dry sherry
**1 cup (140g) slivered
   almonds, toasted**
6 sheets frozen shortcrust pastry
1 egg, beaten
vegetable oil, for deep-frying

SALSA ROJA
400g can tomatoes
5 small fresh red chillies, chopped
1 1/2 cups (375ml) water
2 tablespoons tomato paste
2 cloves garlic, crushed
1 teaspoon sugar

SPICED PEPITAS
20g butter
1 cup (160g) pepitas
1/2 teaspoon chilli powder
1 tablespoon Worcestershire sauce

Place lamb in large pan, cover with cold water; bring to boil. Simmer, covered, for about 1 1/2 hours or until very tender. Drain lamb; discard cooking liquid. Place cooled lamb in large bowl; using fork, shred finely.

Heat peanut oil in large pan; cook garlic, sugar and spices, stirring, until garlic is soft. Stir in juice, sherry, almonds and lamb; remove from heat. *[Can be made ahead to this stage. Cover; refrigerate overnight or freeze.]*

Cut 12cm rounds from pastry sheets (you should get 4 rounds from each sheet). Centre 1 rounded tablespoon of filling on each round; brush around edge with egg, fold over and press together to seal. *[Can be made 3 hours ahead to this stage. Cover empanadas tightly with plastic wrap; refrigerate.]*

Heat vegetable oil in large pan; deep-fry empanadas, in batches, until crisp and browned lightly; drain on absorbent paper. Serve immediately with Salsa Roja and Spiced Pepitas.

Salsa Roja Blend or process undrained tomatoes and remaining ingredients until pureed; transfer to small pan. Bring to boil; simmer about 10 minutes or until sauce thickens. *[Can be made 1 day ahead. Cover; refrigerate.]*

Spiced Pepitas Heat butter in medium pan; cook pepitas and powder, stirring, about 5 minutes or until all pepitas pop. Stir in sauce. *[Can be made 1 day ahead. Cover; refrigerate.]*

MAKES 24

LAMB KOFTA

- 1 tablespoon ghee
- 1 medium (150g) onion, chopped finely
- 2 cloves garlic, crushed
- 1 tablespoon ground cumin
- 1 tablespoon ground coriander
- 1 tablespoon chilli powder
- 2 teaspoons mustard powder
- 1/2 teaspoon ground clove
- 1/2 teaspoon ground nutmeg
- 1kg minced lamb
- 1/2 cup (35g) dried breadcrumbs
- 1 egg, beaten
- 1/3 cup (45g) slivered almonds
- 1/2 cup (75g) dried apricots, chopped
- 1/3 cup finely chopped fresh coriander leaves
- 1/3 cup finely chopped fresh mint leaves
- 200ml yogurt
- 1 tablespoon lime juice
- 1/2 teaspoon ground cardamom

Heat ghee in small pan; cook onion, garlic and spices, stirring, until onion is soft.

Using hands, combine cooled onion mixture in large bowl with the lamb, breadcrumbs, egg, nuts, apricots and half the herbs; roll level tablespoons of kofta mixture into balls. Place on oiled baking tray, cover; refrigerate 1 hour. *[Can be made ahead to this stage. Cover; refrigerate overnight or freeze.]*

Bake kofta, uncovered, in hot oven about 10 minutes or until browned and cooked through. Serve accompanied by combined remaining ingredients.

SERVES 6 TO 8

Opposite Pastitsio
Top right Empanadas with salsa roja and spiced pepitas
Right Lamb kofta

Plate from Accoutrement

SUMAC-CRUMBED CUTLETS WITH CRUNCHY POTATO SALSA

12 French-trimmed lamb cutlets
1/4 cup plain flour
1 egg, beaten
1/2 cup (50g) packaged
    breadcrumbs
1 tablespoon finely grated
    lemon rind
1 tablespoon sumac
2 teaspoons cracked black pepper
1/3 cup (80ml) vegetable oil

CRUNCHY POTATO SALSA
4 medium (800g) potatoes
2 tablespoons olive oil
4 cloves garlic, crushed
1 large (300g) red onion, chopped
2 large (500g) tomatoes,
    seeded, chopped
1 tablespoon lemon juice

Toss cutlets in flour; shake off excess. Dip cutlets in egg then coat with combined breadcrumbs, rind, sumac and pepper. Cover; refrigerate 20 minutes.

Heat oil in large pan; cook cutlets, in batches, until browned both sides and cooked as desired. Drain on absorbent paper; keep warm until ready to serve with Crunchy Potato Salsa.

Crunchy Potato Salsa Dice potatoes into small cubes. Heat half the oil in large pan; cook potato and garlic, stirring, until potato is browned and crisp. Just before serving, toss potato mixture in large bowl with combined onion, tomato, juice and remaining oil.

SERVES 4

Pewter bowl from Accoutrement

LAMB AND VEGETABLE STEW

We used lamb cut from a trimmed forequarter for this recipe.

2 tablespoons olive oil
1kg diced lamb
1 medium (150g) onion, chopped
2 cloves garlic, crushed
3 medium (360g) carrots, chopped
2 sticks (150g) trimmed
    celery, sliced
2 tablespoons instant gravy mix
3 cups (750ml) water
3 large (900g) potatoes, chopped
2 tablespoons finely chopped
    fresh thyme
3/4 cup (90g) frozen peas, thawed

Heat half the oil in large pan; cook lamb, in batches, until browned all over. Heat remaining oil in same pan; cook onion and garlic, stirring, until onion is soft.

Return lamb to pan with carrot and celery; stir in combined gravy mix and water. Bring to boil; simmer, covered, 1 hour, stirring occasionally. *[Can be made ahead to this stage. Cover; refrigerate overnight or freeze.]*

Add potato and thyme; simmer, covered, 30 minutes or until potato is just tender. Stir in peas during last 5 minutes of cooking time.

SERVES 4 TO 6

LAMB WITH FREEKEH PILAU

Roasted greenwheat freekeh is now available in 400g boxes at most supermarkets. We used lamb minced from a trimmed shoulder in this recipe.

2 tablespoons olive oil
1 cup (165g) cracked grain freekeh
1 medium (150g) onion, chopped
1 clove garlic, crushed
1 tablespoon garam masala
1 tablespoon ground cumin
1 tablespoon ground coriander
750g minced lamb
$^{1}/_{4}$ cup (35g) slivered
   almonds, toasted
$^{1}/_{4}$ cup (35g) pistachios,
   toasted, chopped
1$^{3}/_{4}$ cups (430ml) chicken stock
$^{1}/_{4}$ cup firmly packed fresh
   coriander leaves
1 medium (190g) tomato, chopped
200ml yogurt

Heat half the oil in large pan; cook freekeh, stirring, 2 minutes. Transfer freekeh to small bowl.

Heat remaining oil in same pan; cook onion, garlic and spices, stirring, until onion is soft. Add lamb; cook, stirring, until just browned. Return freekeh to pan; stir in nuts and stock. Bring to boil; simmer, covered, 25 minutes or until freekeh is tender and most liquid is absorbed. *[Can be made ahead to this stage. Cover; refrigerate overnight.]* Just before serving, stir in coriander; serve, accompanied by combined tomato and yogurt.

SERVES 4

Copper pot from Accoutrement

Opposite above Sumac-crumbed cutlets with crunchy potato salsa
Opposite below Lamb and vegetable stew
Right Lamb with freekeh pilau

GRILLED CURRIED CUTLETS WITH TOMATO CHICKPEA SALAD

12 French-trimmed lamb cutlets
1/4 cup (60ml) yogurt
2 cloves garlic
1 teaspoon garam masala
1/4 teaspoon chilli powder
1/2 teaspoon ground cumin

LEMON YOGURT SAUCE

3/4 cup (180ml) yogurt
1 tablespoon lemon juice
1 tablespoon water
1 teaspoon ground cumin
1 clove garlic, crushed
1 tablespoon chopped fresh coriander leaves

TOMATO CHICKPEA SALAD

2 x 300g cans chickpeas, drained
2 medium (380g) tomatoes, seeded, chopped
1 medium (170g) red onion, chopped finely
1 tablespoon olive oil
2 tablespoons lemon juice
2 teaspoons chopped fresh coriander leaves
2 cloves garlic, crushed

Toss lamb in large bowl with combined yogurt, garlic and spices; cover, refrigerate several hours or overnight. *[Can be made ahead to this stage. Cover; refrigerate for up to 2 days or freeze.]*

Remove lamb; discard marinade. Cook lamb on heated oiled griddle (or grill or barbecue) until browned both sides and cooked as desired. Served drizzled with Lemon Yogurt Sauce, accompanied by Tomato Chickpea Salad.

Lemon Yogurt Sauce Whisk ingredients together in small bowl. *[Can be made 1 day ahead. Cover; refrigerate.]*

Tomato Chickpea Salad Combine all ingredients in medium bowl. *[Can be made 1 day ahead. Cover; refrigerate.]*

SERVES 4

MANTU

Mantu, a Turkish variation on the meat-filled pasta theme, lusciously confirm why the food of the sultans is considered one of the world's greatest classic cuisines.

2 cups (300g) plain flour
1 egg, beaten
1/3 cup (80ml) water
1 tablespoon milk
2 teaspoons olive oil
20g butter
1 1/2 cups (375ml) chicken stock
200ml yogurt
3 cloves garlic, crushed

LAMB FILLING

450g minced lamb
1 medium (150g) onion, grated
2 teaspoons finely chopped fresh oregano
1 teaspoon ground cumin
2 teaspoons tomato paste
1/2 teaspoon cracked black pepper

Process flour, egg, water, milk and oil until mixture forms a ball. Transfer dough to floured surface; knead for about 10 minutes or until smooth. Divide dough into quarters; roll each piece through pasta machine set on thickest setting. Fold dough in half, roll through machine. Repeat rolling several times, adjusting setting so pasta sheets become thinner with each roll; dust pasta with extra flour when necessary. Roll to second thinnest setting (1mm thick), making sure pasta is at least 10cm wide.

Cut pasta into 5cm squares. Centre 1 level teaspoon of filling on each square; pinch corners together then press sides together to form a pyramid shape. Place tightly together in oiled large ovenproof dish; brush with melted butter. *[Can be made 3 hours ahead to this stage. Cover tightly with plastic wrap; refrigerate.]*

Bake mantu, uncovered, in moderate oven about 30 minutes or until tops are browned slightly. Pour hot stock over mantu; bake, uncovered, about 15 minutes or until almost all liquid is absorbed. Serve with blended yogurt and garlic.

Lamb Filling Combine all ingredients in medium bowl. *[Can be made 1 day ahead. Cover; refrigerate.]*

SERVES 4 TO 6

Opposite Grilled curried cutlets with tomato chickpea salad
Below Mantu, Turkish meat-filled pasta

China and stemware from Waterford Wedgwood

BRAINS WITH BLACK BUTTER

4 sets lamb brains
1 teaspoon salt
¼ cup (35g) flour
125g butter
1 large (500g) leek, sliced
1 tablespoon brown sugar
2 cloves garlic, crushed
150g button mushrooms, quartered
2 teaspoons finely fresh
    tarragon leaves

Place brains in large bowl, cover with cold water; gently stir in the salt. Cover; refrigerate overnight.

Drain brains; halve each set. Using scissors, carefully remove membranes and veins. Place brains in medium pan, cover with cold water; bring to boil, uncovered, then simmer, uncovered, 2 minutes. Drain brains; discard cooking liquid. Pat brains dry with absorbent paper; toss in flour.

Heat a third of the butter in large pan; cook leek, stirring, until browned and soft. Stir in sugar until dissolved; remove leek mixture from pan, cover to keep warm.

Heat half the remaining butter in same pan; cook garlic and mushrooms, stirring, until mushrooms are tender. Stir in tarragon; remove mushroom mixture from pan, cover to keep warm.

Heat remaining butter in same pan until it foams; cook brains, uncovered, until browned both sides and cooked through. Add mushroom mixture; stir gently to combine. Serve immediately on hot leek mixture.

SERVES 4

LIVER AND BACON

4 bacon rashers
500g lamb liver
2 tablespoons plain flour
½ teaspoon cracked black pepper
1 tablespoon olive oil
20g butter
2 cloves garlic, crushed
1 tablespoon Worcestershire sauce
2 green onions, sliced thinly
1 tablespoon chopped fresh parsley

Cook bacon, uncovered, in large dry heated pan until browned and crisp; drain on absorbent paper.

Remove and discard membrane and any fat from liver; slice thinly. Toss in combined flour and pepper, shake off excess. Heat oil and butter in same pan; cook liver, uncovered, about 2 minutes or until browned all over and cooked as desired. Add garlic and sauce; cook, stirring, 1 minute. Serve liver with bacon; sprinkle with onion and parsley.

SERVES 4

China from Accoutrement

HONEY MUSTARD PARTY RACK

A "party" rack of lamb is an uncut whole rack, averaging 13 ribs in total.

¹/₃ cup honey
1¹/₂ tablespoons seeded mustard
2 cloves garlic, crushed
1 teaspoon soy sauce
2 teaspoons lime juice
2 lamb party racks (13 cutlets to each rack)

Combine honey, mustard, garlic, sauce and juice in large bowl; add lamb, coat in marinade. Cover; refrigerate 3 hours or overnight. *[Can be refrigerated, covered, up to 2 days, or frozen, at this stage.]*

Place lamb racks in large oiled baking dish; reserve marinade. Bake racks, covered, in hot oven 15 minutes. Brush racks with reserved marinade; bake, uncovered, about 20 minutes or until browned all over and cooked as desired.

SERVES 4 TO 6

Opposite above Liver and bacon
Opposite Brains with black butter
Above Honey mustard party rack

Plates from Corso De' Fiori

LAMB SOUVLAKIA

Soak bamboo skewers in water for at least 1 hour or overnight to prevent scorching. We used lamb cut from a trimmed leg.

- **¼ cup (60ml) olive oil**
- **1 teaspoon finely grated lemon rind**
- **¼ cup (60ml) lemon juice**
- **2 cloves garlic, crushed**
- **1 tablespoon finely chopped fresh oregano**
- **1 small (80g) onion, chopped finely**
- **1kg diced lamb**
- **1 cup (160g) black olives, seeded**
- **1 large (250g) tomato, chopped**
- **150g firm fetta cheese, chopped**
- **1 tablespoon olive oil, extra**

Combine oil, rind, juice, garlic, oregano and onion in large bowl; add lamb, coat in marinade. Cover; refrigerate 3 hours or overnight. *[Can be refrigerated, covered, up to 2 days, or frozen, at this stage.]*

Thread lamb onto 12 bamboo skewers; cook skewers, in batches, on heated oiled griddle (or grill or barbecue) until browned all over and cooked as desired.

Serve accompanied by combined remaining ingredients.

SERVES 4 TO 6

MOUSSAKA

- **3 large (1.5kg) eggplants**
- **¹/₃ cup olive oil**
- **2 large (400g) onions, chopped finely**
- **4 cloves garlic, crushed**
- **1kg minced lamb**
- **425g can tomatoes**
- **¼ cup tomato paste**
- **½ cup (125ml) dry red wine**
- **2 tablespoons finely chopped fresh parsley**
- **½ teaspoon ground cinnamon**
- **¼ teaspoon ground clove**
- **½ teaspoon ground nutmeg**

CHEESE SAUCE
- **125g butter**
- **²/₃ cup plain flour**
- **1 litre (4 cups) milk**
- **½ cup (40g) coarsely grated parmesan cheese**
- **2 eggs**

Cut eggplant into 5mm slices, sprinkle all over with salt; stand, in single layer, 20 minutes. Rinse eggplant thoroughly under cold water; drain. Pat dry with absorbent paper. Place eggplant slices, in single layer, on oiled oven trays. Brush with a little of the oil; cook, 1 side only, on heated oiled griddle (or grill or barbecue) until browned lightly; drain on absorbent paper. *[Can be made ahead to*

Casserole from Accoutrement

this stage. Cover tightly with plastic wrap; refrigerate overnight.]

Heat 2 tablespoons of remaining oil in large pan; cook onion and garlic, stirring, until onion is soft. Add lamb; cook, stirring, until lamb is browned and cooked through. Add undrained crushed tomatoes, paste, wine, parsley, cinnamon and clove; season to taste with salt and pepper, if desired. Bring to boil; simmer, covered, 30 minutes. *[Can be made ahead to this stage. Cover; refrigerate overnight.]*

Oil shallow 3-litre (12-cup) ovenproof dish. Line dish with a third of the eggplant; top with half the meat sauce, half the remaining eggplant, remaining meat sauce, then remaining eggplant. Spread Cheese Sauce over top, sprinkle with nutmeg. Bake, uncovered, in moderate oven about 45 minutes or until Cheese Sauce sets and is browned lightly.

Cheese Sauce Heat butter in large pan; cook flour, stirring, about 1 minute or until bubbling. Remove from heat; gradually stir in milk. Return to heat; cook, stirring, until sauce boils and thickens. Cool 5 minutes; stir in combined cheese and eggs.

SERVES 6

Opposite above Lamb souvlakia
Opposite Moussaka
Below Thelma's baked kibbeh

THELMA'S BAKED KIBBEH

Kibbeh is most flavoursome when made from lamb shoulder which has had as much gristle, fat and sinew as possible removed before being minced. If you own a meat mincer, grind the meat yourself to get the right degree of both coarse and fine mince.

1¹/₂ cups (240g) burghul
2 teaspoons salt
1 large (200g) brown onion, chopped finely
500g finely minced lamb
1 teaspoon ground black pepper
1 teaspoon ground allspice
¹/₂ cup iced water
1 tablespoon (15g) butter
¹/₂ cup (125ml) olive oil

FILLING

2 teaspoons olive oil
250g coarsely minced lamb
1 medium (150g) brown onion, chopped finely
1 teaspoon allspice
¹/₂ teaspoon ground cinnamon
¹/₂ teaspoon ground nutmeg
1 teaspoon salt
¹/₂ teaspoon ground white pepper
³/₄ cup (130g) pine nuts, toasted

Oil a 25cm x 32cm baking dish. Cover burghul with cold water in medium bowl; stand for 10 minutes. Sprinkle salt over onion; stand 10 minutes. Drain burghul, squeezing with hands to remove as much water as possible. Rinse onion under cold water; squeeze dry in absorbent paper. Combine burghul, onion, lamb, pepper, allspice and water in large bowl; knead about 10 minutes or until mixture forms a smooth paste. (To ensure kibbeh mixture stays cold and smooth, knead in a small piece of ice from time to time.)

Divide kibbeh mixture in half. Using wet hands, press half the kibbeh mixture over base of prepared dish, smoothing surface to ensure base is covered evenly. Drain and discard excess oil from Filling then spread Filling evenly over kibbeh layer in dish. Shape the remaining burghul mixture into large, thin patties. Place patties over Filling layer to cover as much as possible then, using wet hands, carefully join patties to ensure Filling is completely covered. Gently smooth top with wet hands then, using wet knife, cut through kibbeh to form diamond shapes. Dot each diamond with a pinch of the butter. *[Can be made ahead to this stage. Cover; refrigerate overnight.]*

Drizzle kibbeh with oil, particularly into cut pattern and around dish sides. Bake, uncovered, in moderate oven about 1¹/₂ hours or until kibbeh is browned and cooked through. Drain away excess oil before serving.

Filling Heat oil in medium pan; cook lamb, stirring, over high heat, until browned. Add onion; cook, stirring, until browned lightly. Stir in spices, salt and pepper; remove from heat, stir in nuts.

SERVES 6 TO 8

Tray from Home & Garden on the Mall

THAI GREEN CURRY

1 tablespoon vegetable oil
1kg diced lamb
1 large (200g) onion, sliced
1/3 cup (80G) green curry paste
3 cups (750ml) chicken stock
2 bay leaves
1 2/3 cups (410ml) coconut cream
1 large (350g) green capsicum,
    sliced thinly
100g snow peas, trimmed
425g can whole baby corn, drained
2 tablespoons finely chopped fresh
    coriander leaves
1/2 cup (40g) bean sprouts

Heat oil in large pan; cook lamb, in batches, until browned all over. Add onion and curry paste to same pan; cook, stirring, until onion is soft. Return lamb to pan; add stock and bay leaves. Bring to boil; simmer, uncovered, 1 1/2 hours or until lamb is tender. [Can be made ahead to this stage. Cover; refrigerate overnight or freeze.] Add cream, capsicum, snow peas, corn and coriander; stir until heated through. Serve topped with sprouts.

SERVES 4 TO 6

ROGAN JOSH WITH CASHEW BANANA RAITA

We used trimmed lamb shoulder for this recipe. On average, 2 large, overripe bananas makes 1 cup mashed banana.

2 tablespoons peanut oil
800g diced lamb
4 cloves garlic, crushed
1 large (300g) red onion, chopped
3 small fresh red chillies,
    seeded, chopped
2 teaspoons ground cumin
1 teaspoon ground cardamom
1 teaspoon ground clove
2 teaspoons ground ginger
1/4 cup poppy seeds
1 cinnamon stick
4 small (400g) tomatoes, chopped
415g can tomato puree
1 cup (250ml) yogurt

CASHEW BANANA RAITA

1 cup (250ml) yogurt
1/4 cup (35g) chopped
    roasted cashews
1 cup mashed banana

Heat oil in large pan; cook lamb, stirring, in batches, until browned all over.

Add garlic, onion, chilli, spices, seeds and cinnamon stick to same pan; cook, stirring, until onion is soft. Return lamb to pan; add tomato and puree. Bring to boil; simmer, covered, about 1 hour or until tender. [Can be made ahead to this stage. Cover; refrigerate overnight or freeze.]

Just before serving, stir in whisked yogurt; serve with Cashew Banana Raita.

Cashew Banana Raita Combine all ingredients in small bowl; cover, refrigerate 30 minutes. [Can be made 3 hours ahead. Cover; refrigerate.]

SERVES 4 TO 6

Opposite Thai green curry
Above Rogan josh with cashew banana raita

Casserole from Accoutrement

NAVARIN OF LAMB

1.5kg lamb shoulder,
  trimmed, diced
3 cloves garlic, crushed
1/4 cup (35g) plain flour
2 tablespoons vegetable oil
1 cup (250ml) chicken stock
1/2 cup (125ml) dry white wine
1 tablespoon tomato paste
10 baby (250g) onions
1 sprig fresh rosemary
2 sprigs fresh thyme
2 bay leaves
1 bunch (300g) baby carrots
4 small (360g) turnips, quartered
2 tablespoons roughly chopped
  fresh flat-leaf parsley

Toss lamb in large bowl with garlic and
flour. Heat oil in large pan; cook lamb, in
batches, until just browned. Return lamb
to pan; add stock, wine, paste, onions,
fresh herbs and bay leaves. Bring to boil;
simmer, covered, 1³/4 hours. Add carrots
and turnips; simmer, covered, about
45 minutes or until lamb and vegetables
are tender. *[Can be made ahead to this
stage. Cover; refrigerate overnight.]* Just
before serving, stir in parsley.

SERVES 6

OLD-FASHIONED LAMB
AND VEGETABLE PIE

We used lamb from a trimmed leg in this pie.

1¹/2 cups (225g) plain flour
125g cold butter, chopped
1 egg yolk
1 tablespoon iced water,
  approximately
1 sheet ready-rolled puff pastry
1 egg, beaten

LAMB FILLING
2 tablespoons olive oil
750g diced lamb
1 large (200g) onion, sliced
2 cloves garlic, crushed
1 large (500g) leek, chopped
2 sticks (150g) trimmed
  celery, sliced
1 large (180g) carrot, chopped
400g can tomatoes
1/4 cup (60ml) Worcestershire sauce
1/4 cup (60ml) barbecue sauce
1/2 cup (125ml) beef stock
1 cup (125g) frozen peas

Oil 20cm springform tin. Process flour and
butter until crumbly; add egg yolk and
enough water to make ingredients just
cling together. Transfer dough to floured
surface; knead until smooth. Wrap dough
in plastic; refrigerate 30 minutes.

Roll dough between sheets of baking paper until large enough to line prepared tin. Lift pastry into tin, press into side, trim edge; refrigerate 30 minutes.

Place tin on oven tray, bake blind, uncovered, in moderately hot oven about 20 minutes or until browned lightly; cool.

Spoon cold Lamb Filling into pastry case. Brush edge with egg; top pie with puff pastry sheet, gently press to seal, trim edge. Brush pie with egg; decorate with pastry scraps, if desired. Bake, uncovered, in moderately hot oven about 30 minutes or until browned.

Lamb Filling Heat half the oil in large pan; cook lamb, in batches, stirring, until browned all over. Heat remaining oil in same pan; cook onion, garlic, leek, celery and carrot; cook, stirring until vegetables are just soft. Add undrained crushed tomatoes, sauces and stock. Bring to boil; simmer, covered, about 1 hour or until lamb is tender. Uncover; simmer, stirring occasionally, about 30 minutes or until mixture thickens. Add peas during final 5 minutes of cooking time. *[Can be made ahead. Cover; refrigerate overnight.]*

SERVES 4 TO 6

LAMB SHANKS WITH SESAME-FRIED POLENTA

French-trimmed lamb shanks are called "drumsticks" by some butchers, the shanks having been trimmed of all sinew and fat so that they resemble a gigantic chicken leg.

8 lamb drumsticks
1 tablespoon Worcestershire sauce
2 tablespoons light soy sauce
2 tablespoons barbecue sauce
4 cloves garlic
1/2 teaspoon cracked black pepper
1 teaspoon sesame oil
1 tablespoon finely chopped fresh oregano
1 tablespoon finely chopped fresh basil leaves
1 tablespoon finely chopped fresh rosemary

SESAME-FRIED POLENTA
3 cups water
1 1/2 cups (250g) polenta
1 tablespoon (15g) butter
1/3 cup (25g) finely grated parmesan cheese
1 teaspoon cracked black pepper
1/4 cup plain flour
1 egg, lightly beaten
1 cup sesame seeds
1/3 cup (80ml) vegetable oil

Plate from Accoutrement

Toss drumsticks in large bowl with combined sauces, garlic, pepper, oil and herbs; cover, refrigerate several hours or overnight. *[Can be made ahead to this stage. Cover; refrigerate up to 2 days or freeze.]*

Drain drumsticks; reserve marinade. Place drumsticks in large shallow oiled baking dish. Bake, covered, in moderate oven for 1 hour. Brush drumsticks with reserved marinade; bake, uncovered, 30 minutes, brushing occasionally with reserved marinade. Serve with Sesame-Fried Polenta.

Sesame-Fried Polenta Oil 19cm x 29cm slice pan; line base with baking paper, extending the paper 2cm over edges of both long sides.

Bring water to boil in large pan; reduce heat, gradually whisk in polenta. Cook, stirring, over medium heat, about 10 minutes or until mixture thickens; stir in butter, cheese and pepper. Spoon polenta into prepared pan; press firmly to ensure even thickness. When cool, cover; refrigerate until firm. *[Can be made ahead to this stage. Cover; refrigerate up to 2 days or freeze.]*

Turn polenta onto board, trim edges; cut into 12 large pieces, cut each piece into 2 triangles. Coat polenta in flour, shake off excess. Brush with beaten egg; toss in large bowl with seeds to coat; Place polenta on tray; cover, refrigerate 20 minutes. *[Can be made 1 day ahead.]*

Heat oil in large pan; cook polenta, in batches, until browned lightly both sides. Drain on absorbent paper.

SERVES 4

Opposite above Navarin of lamb
Opposite Old-fashioned lamb and vegetable pie
Above Lamb shanks with sesame-fried polenta

DEVILLED KIDNEYS

12 lamb kidneys
1 teaspoon salt
$1/4$ cup (60ml) Worcestershire sauce
2 tablespoons tomato sauce
1 tablespoon barbecue sauce
$1/4$ teaspoon hot paprika
$1/2$ teaspoon sugar
2 teaspoons Dijon mustard
1 cup (250ml) beef stock
30g butter
1 tablespoon vegetable oil
1 tablespoon plain flour
1 tablespoon finely
    chopped fresh parsley

Remove skin and fat from kidneys; cover with cold water in large bowl, stir in salt. Cover; refrigerate overnight.

Drain kidneys; rinse under cold water, drain. Halve kidneys lengthways, remove and discard core of fat; slice kidneys thinly.

Combine sauces, paprika, sugar, mustard and stock in small bowl. Heat butter and oil in large pan; cook kidney, uncovered, over high heat, until browned all over and just cooked through. Remove from pan; cover to keep warm.

Add flour to same pan; cook, stirring, 1 minute. Add sauce mixture; cook, stirring, until mixture boils and thickens. Return kidney to pan; stir until heated through. Just before serving, sprinkle with parsley.

SERVES 4

LAHEM B'AJEEN

Sometimes called ladies' fingers, these lamb and pine nut fillo-wrapped "cigars" make perfect pre-dinner snacks.

1 tablespoon olive oil
500g minced lamb
2 cloves garlic, crushed
$1/2$ teaspoon cracked black pepper
$1/2$ teaspoon ground cinnamon
2 teaspoons mixed spice
$1/2$ cup (80g) pine nuts,
    toasted, chopped
1 tablespoon lemon juice
14 sheets (210g) fillo pastry
5 tablespoons ghee

Left Devilled kidneys
Above Lamb fricassee
Right Lahem b'ajeen, ladies' fingers

LAMB FRICASSEE

- 1 tablespoon vegetable oil
- 2 medium (700g) leeks, sliced
- 2 large (400g) onions, sliced
- 2 cloves garlic, crushed
- 1/4 cup (35g) plain flour
- 12 lamb neck chops
- 1/4 cup (60ml) dry white wine
- 3 cups (750ml) chicken stock
- 2 bay leaves
- 1 tablespoon finely chopped
  fresh parsley
- 1 teaspoon finely chopped fresh dill
- 1 teaspoon cracked black pepper
- 2 egg yolks
- 1/2 cup (125ml) cream
- 1 tablespoon lemon juice
- 1/4 teaspoon ground nutmeg
- 1/4 teaspoon ground cinnamon

Heat oil in large pan; cook leek, onion and garlic, stirring, until leek is soft. Add flour; cook, stirring, 1 minute. Add lamb, wine, stock and leaves. Bring to boil; simmer, covered, about 1 hour or until lamb is tender. Stir in parsley, dill and pepper; simmer, uncovered, for about 15 minutes or until sauce thickens slightly. *[Can be made ahead to this stage. Cover; refrigerate overnight or freeze.]*

Just before serving, stir in combined egg yolks, cream, juice, nutmeg and cinnamon; cook over low heat, stirring, until hot.

SERVES 4 TO 6

Heat oil in large pan; cook lamb, stirring, until browned and cooked through. Add garlic, pepper, cinnamon, mixed spice and nuts; cook, stirring, about 1 minute or until liquid is almost evaporated. Stir in juice. *[Can be made ahead to this stage. Cover; refrigerate overnight or freeze.]*

Halve stack of fillo sheets lengthways; to prevent pastry drying out, cover with damp tea-towel. Working with 1 half-sheet at a time, brush fillo with melted ghee; place 1 level tablespoon cooled lamb mixture along 1 narrow end of fillo. Roll fillo into tight cigar-shape; to enclose filling, fold in sides of fillo as you roll. Repeat with remaining pieces of fillo and lamb mixture.

Place lahem b'ajeen 2cm apart on oiled oven trays; brush each lahem b'ajeen all over with remaining melted ghee. *[Can be made 3 hours ahead to this stage. Cover tightly with plastic wrap; refrigerate.]*

Bake, uncovered, in hot oven for about 10 minutes or until brown and crisp.

MAKES 28

IRISH STEW
WITH HERB DUMPLINGS

*We used meat cut from a trimmed
lamb shoulder for this recipe.*

1kg diced lamb
2 tablespoons plain flour
1 teaspoon freshly ground
   black pepper
2 large (400g) onions, sliced
2 large (600g) potatoes, sliced
1 large (180g) carrot, sliced
1/2 cup (100g) pearl barley
2 teaspoons finely chopped
   fresh thyme
11/2 cups (375ml) lamb or
   vegetable stock
1 litre (4 cups) hot water

HERB DUMPLINGS
1 cup (150g) self-raising flour
50g cold butter, chopped
1 tablespoon finely chopped
   fresh parsley
1 tablespoon finely chopped
   fresh thyme
1 egg, beaten
1/4 cup (60ml) milk, approximately

Toss lamb in large bowl with combined
flour and pepper.

Layer half the onion, potato, carrot
and lamb in large heavy-based pan;
repeat layering with the remaining
vegetables and lamb. Sprinkle with barley
and thyme; pour over combined stock and
water. Bring to boil; skim surface of stew.
Simmer, covered, for 11/2 hours. *[Can be
made ahead to this stage. Cover;
refrigerate overnight.]*

Uncover stew; drop heaped tablespoons dumpling mixture, 2cm apart, on
top. Cover stew; simmer about 15 minutes
or until dumplings are cooked through.

Herb Dumplings Sift flour into medium
bowl; rub in butter. Stir in herbs, egg and
enough milk to mix to a soft, sticky dough.

SERVES 4 TO 6

Copper pot from The Bay Tree Kitchen Shop

AUSHAK

Aushak are the Afghan version of Italian ravioli — leek, mint and yogurt make a refreshing addition to these pillows.

1 cup (150g) plain flour
1 teaspoon salt
2 teaspoons olive oil
1/3 cup (80ml) cold water
200ml yogurt
2 tablespoons finely shredded fresh mint leaves

LEEK FILLING
1 tablespoon olive oil
2 large (1kg) leeks, sliced thinly
2 cloves garlic, crushed
1/2 teaspoon hot paprika

MEAT SAUCE
1/4 cup (60ml) olive oil
1 medium (150g) onion, finely chopped
500g minced lamb
1 cup (250ml) lamb or beef stock
1/4 cup (60ml) tomato paste
2 teaspoons mixed spice
1 teaspoon cracked black pepper

Process flour, salt, oil and water until mixture forms a ball. Transfer dough to floured surface; knead until smooth. Divide dough in half; roll each piece through pasta machine set on thickest setting. Fold dough in half, roll through machine. Repeat rolling several times, adjusting setting so pasta sheets become thinner with each roll; dust pasta with extra flour when necessary. Roll to second thinnest setting (1mm thick), making sure pasta is at least 12cm wide.

Cut pasta into 5.5cm rounds. Centre 1 level teaspoon Leek Filling on each round; brush around edge with water, fold over and press together to seal. *[Can be made 3 hours ahead to this stage. Cover tightly with plastic wrap; refrigerate.]*

Cook aushak, in batches, in large pan of boiling water, uncovered, until just tender; remove carefully, using slotted spoon. Drain; serve immediately topped with Meat Sauce, whisked yogurt and mint.

Leek Filling Heat oil in large pan; cook leeks, garlic and paprika, stirring, until leeks are very soft and lightly browned. Cool to room temperature. *[Can be made ahead. Cover; refrigerate overnight.]*

Meat Sauce Heat oil in large pan; cook onion, stirring, until soft. Add lamb; cook, stirring, until browned. Stir in stock, paste, mixed spice and pepper. Bring to boil; simmer, uncovered, about 20 minutes or until sauce thickens. *[Can be made ahead. Cover; refrigerate overnight.]*

SERVES 4

LAMB AND QUINCE TAGINE

Some butchers call lamb drumsticks "French-trimmed lamb shanks" because drumsticks are shanks with as much gristle, sinew and fat as possible removed.

2 medium (300g) onions
1 tablespoon olive oil
80g butter
1 tablespoon ground cumin
1 1/2 teaspoons ground ginger
1 teaspoon sweet paprika
1/2 teaspoon ground cinnamon
1 cinnamon stick
8 lamb drumsticks
2 1/2 cups (625ml) water
2 tablespoons tomato paste
3 (1kg) quinces
1 1/2 tablespoons lemon juice
1 tablespoon honey
1/4 cup roughly chopped fresh coriander leaves

Cut onions into wedges. Heat oil and half the butter in large heavy-based pan; cook onions, stirring, about 5 minutes or until browned lightly. Add ground spices and cinnamon stick; cook, stirring, until fragrant. Add lamb, water and paste; bring to boil, stirring. Simmer, covered, 1 1/4 hours, stirring occasionally. *[Can be made ahead to this stage. Cover; refrigerate overnight or freeze.]* Remove lamb only from pan; cover, on serving plate, to keep warm.

Meanwhile, peel and quarter quinces; remove and discard cores then cut each quarter into thirds. Heat remaining butter in separate pan; cook quince, stirring, about 6 minutes or until browned lightly.

Add quince to pan with onion-spice mixture, bring to boil; simmer, covered, 20 minutes. Add juice, honey and half the coriander; simmer, uncovered, 10 minutes. Spoon quinces and pan juices over lamb; sprinkle with remaining coriander.

SERVES 4

Above Lamb and quince tagine
Top right Aushak, Afghan ravioli
Right Lamb korma

LAMB KORMA

We used meat that was cut from a trimmed leg of lamb for this recipe.

1 tablespoon peanut oil
1 large fresh red chilli, seeded, chopped finely
2 large (400g) onions, sliced finely
3 cloves garlic, crushed
2 tablespoons grated fresh ginger
1 tablespoon ground cumin
3 teaspoons ground coriander
1¹/₂ teaspoons garam masala
1.5kg diced lamb
1²/₃ cups (410ml) coconut milk
200ml yogurt
400g can tomatoes
6 cardamom pods, bruised
1 cinnamon stick
¹/₃ cup (25g) flaked almonds, toasted
1 tablespoon tamarind concentrate

Heat oil in large pan; cook chilli, onion, garlic, ginger and spices, stirring, until onion is soft. Stir lamb into spice mixture; add combined coconut milk and yogurt gradually, stirring well between each addition. Add undrained crushed tomatoes, pods and cinnamon stick, bring to boil; simmer, covered, 1 hour. Uncover; simmer, stirring occasionally about 1 hour or until lamb is tender. *[Can be made ahead to this stage. Cover; refrigerate overnight.]* Just before serving, stir in almonds and tamarind.

SERVES 4 TO 6

LAMB TAGINE WITH FRUIT AND NUT COUSCOUS

1 large (500g) eggplant
1 tablespoon olive oil
1kg diced lamb
1 large (200g) onion, sliced
2 cloves garlic, crushed
1/2 teaspoon ground cinnamon
1 tablespoon ground cumin
2 teaspoons ground coriander
1 teaspoon ground turmeric
1/2 teaspoon ground ginger
4 cardamom pods, bruised
4 x 5cm strips lemon rind
1 litre (4 cups) water
4 medium (480g) zucchini, chopped
2 tablespoons honey
3/4 cup (110g) dried apricots, halved
1 tablespoon finely chopped fresh coriander leaves
2 tablespoons finely chopped fresh mint leaves

FRUIT AND NUT COUSCOUS
2 cups (500ml) water
20g butter
2 cups (400g) couscous
1/2 cup (75g) dried currants
1/2 cup (80g) pine nuts, toasted
2 tablespoons chopped fresh coriander leaves

Place chopped unpeeled eggplant in strainer, sprinkle all over with salt; stand 30 minutes. Rinse eggplant under cold water; drain on absorbent paper.

Heat half the oil in large pan; cook lamb, in batches, until browned all over. Heat remaining oil in same pan; cook onion, garlic, ground spices and pods, stirring, until onion is soft. Return lamb to pan; stir in rind and water. Bring to boil; simmer, covered, 1 hour.

Stir in eggplant, zucchini, honey and apricots; simmer, uncovered, about 30 minutes or until eggplant is tender. *[Can be made ahead to this stage. Cover; refrigerate overnight.]*

Just before serving with Fruit and Nut Couscous, stir in coriander and mint.

Fruit and Nut Couscous Bring water to boil in medium pan; stir in butter and couscous. Remove from heat, cover; stand about 5 minutes, fluffing with fork occasionally, until water is absorbed. Using fork, gently mix in currants, pine nuts and coriander.

SERVES 4 TO 6

LAMB SATAY

We used lamb round roast but a small trimmed boned leg could be substituted.

1kg lamb round roast
2 teaspoons peanut oil
1 tablespoon finely chopped fresh lemon grass
2 teaspoons ground cumin
11/2 cups (375ml) lamb or chicken stock
1/2 cup (130g) smooth peanut butter
1/4 cup (60ml) sweet chilli sauce
2 teaspoons lemon juice
1 tablespoon finely chopped fresh coriander leaves

Cut lamb into 3cm pieces; thread onto 12 skewers.

Heat oil in medium pan; cook lemon grass and cumin, stirring, until fragrant. Add remaining ingredients, bring to boil, stirring; simmer, uncovered, 5 minutes. *[Can be made ahead to this stage. Cover, separately; refrigerate overnight.]*

Cook skewers, in batches, on heated oiled griddle (or grill or barbecue) until browned all over and cooked as desired; serve lamb skewers with hot satay sauce.

SERVES 4 TO 6

Below Lamb tagine with fruit and nut couscous
Right Lamb satay

China from Waterford Wedgwood

SLOW-COOKED LAMB SHOULDER

2 tablespoons olive oil
1.2kg lamb shoulder
2 medium (300g) onions,
  chopped coarsely
2 medium (240g) carrots,
  chopped coarsely
2 sticks (150g) celery,
  chopped coarsely

1 tablespoon sugar
1/2 cup (125ml) dry red wine
1/2 cup (125ml) lamb or beef stock
10 sprigs fresh oregano or rosemary

Heat oil in large flameproof baking dish; cook lamb, uncovered, over high heat until browned all over. Remove lamb from dish. Cook vegetables in same dish, stirring, until browned lightly. Add sugar; cook, stirring, 1 minute. Add wine and stock, bring to boil; remove from heat.

Place half the herbs on vegetables; place lamb on top then place remaining herbs on lamb. Bake, covered tightly, in slow oven 1 1/2 hours. Turn lamb; bake, covered, 1 1/2 hours. Turn again; bake, covered, 1 hour.

Carefully remove lamb from dish; wrap in foil. Strain pan contents, discarding vegetables, herbs and as much fat as possible. Serve lamb with strained hot juice poured over the top.

SERVES 4

LAMB EN CROUTE

We used purchased green peppercorn pate in this recipe but you can substitute it with whatever variety you prefer.

4 x 20cm (1kg) whole pieces lamb eye of loin
20g butter
200g button mushrooms, sliced
100g green peppercorn pate
2 sheets ready-rolled puff pastry
1 egg, beaten

MUSHROOM SAUCE
40g butter
1 large (200g) onion, sliced
2 cloves garlic, crushed
200g field mushrooms, sliced
1 tablespoon brandy
1 tablespoon plain flour
1¹/₂ cups (370ml) lamb or vegetable stock
¹/₂ cup (125ml) cream

Sandwich 2 pieces of lamb together; tie together with kitchen string. Repeat with remaining 2 pieces of lamb. Heat large oiled pan; cook lamb until just browned on all sides.

Meanwhile, heat butter in small pan; cook mushrooms, stirring, until soft. Discard any aspic from pate; using fork, mash pate in small bowl.

Divide pate between pastry sheets, spreading to leave 2cm border; sprinkle equal amounts of mushrooms over each sheet. Remove string from lamb; centre 2 lamb loins on each sheet. Brush egg around edges of sheets, then roll over lamb to form parcels. Brush with remaining egg; place parcels, seam-side down, on oiled oven tray. *[Can be made ahead to this stage. Cover tightly with plastic wrap; refrigerate overnight.]*

Bake in hot oven about 20 minutes or until pastry is browned and crisp, and the lamb is cooked through. Serve with Mushroom Sauce.

Mushroom Sauce Melt butter in medium pan; cook onion, stirring, until browned lightly. Add garlic, mushrooms and brandy; cook, stirring, until mushrooms are soft and liquid has evaporated. Add flour; cook, stirring, until mixture is bubbling. Remove from heat; gradually stir in stock and cream. Bring to boil; simmer, stirring, 5 minutes or until sauce boils and thickens slightly.

SERVES 4 TO 6

Opposite Slow-cooked lamb shoulder
Right Lamb en croute

Plates and glass from The Bay Tree Kitchen Shop

NO-FUSS CASSOULET

You can substitute 2 x 310g cans rinsed and drained cannellini beans for the dried beans; add canned beans just before baking.

1¹/₂ cups (300g) dried
    haricot or navy beans
750g boned leg of lamb
2 tablespoons olive oil
4 (350g) thick pork sausages
250g piece streaky bacon, chopped
1 large (200g) onion, chopped
2 cloves garlic, crushed
2 sticks (150g) trimmed
    celery, chopped
2 medium (240g) carrots, chopped
2 x 400g cans tomatoes
2 cups (500ml) lamb or
    chicken stock
¹/₂ cup (125ml) dry red wine
1 tablespoon finely chopped
    fresh parsley
2 teaspoons finely chopped
    fresh thyme
2 cups (140g) stale breadcrumbs
20g butter

LAMB RENDANG

We used meat cut from a trimmed leg of lamb for this recipe.

4cm piece fresh galangal,
    chopped coarsely
4cm piece fresh ginger,
    chopped coarsely
6 cloves garlic, crushed
3 large fresh red chillies,
    halved, seeded,
4 fresh kaffir lime leaves, torn
1¹/₂ cups (125g) freshly
    grated coconut
1kg diced lamb
2 cinnamon sticks
4 cloves
10 star-anise
6 cardamom pods
2 tablespoons peanut oil
3 cups (750ml) coconut milk
1 cup (250ml) lamb or beef stock
¹/₃ cup (80ml) lime juice
1 tablespoon brown sugar

Blend or process galangal, ginger, garlic, chilli and leaves until crushed finely. Transfer to large bowl; stir in coconut. Add lamb; toss to coat with the coconut mixture. Cover tightly; refrigerate 3 hours or overnight.

Blend or process cinnamon sticks, cloves, star-anise and cardamom until crushed finely. Heat oil in large pan; cook dry spice mixture, stirring, until fragrant. Add lamb mixture; cook, stirring, about 3 minutes or until browned lightly. Stir in milk and stock, bring to boil; simmer, uncovered, stirring occasionally, about 1¹/₄ hours or until lamb is tender. *[Can be made ahead to this stage. Cover; refrigerate overnight or freeze.]*

Stir in juice and sugar, bring to boil; simmer, stirring, about 5 minutes or until sauce thickens slightly.

SERVES 4 TO 6

Cover beans with cold water in large bowl; cover, stand overnight.

Drain beans; rinse under cold water, drain. Add beans to large pan of boiling water; simmer, uncovered, for about 25 minutes or until just tender. Drain; discard cooking liquid.

Cut lamb into 2cm cubes. Heat half the oil in large pan; cook lamb, in batches, until browned all over. Transfer lamb to deep 3-litre (12-cup) ovenproof dish.

Add sausages to same pan; cook, uncovered, until browned all over. Quarter sausages; transfer to dish with lamb.

Heat remaining oil in same pan; cook bacon, onion and garlic, stirring, until onion is soft. Add celery and carrots; cook, stirring, until vegetables are just soft. Transfer vegetable mixture to dish with lamb; stir in beans, undrained crushed tomatoes, stock, wine, parsley and thyme.

Bake, uncovered, in moderately hot oven about 1 hour or until lamb is tender. *[Can be made ahead to this stage. Cover; refrigerate overnight or freeze.]*

Sprinkle cassoulet with breadcrumbs; dot with butter. Bake, uncovered, about 45 minutes or until top is browned.

SERVES 6

Casserole dish from Accoutrement

LAMB RAGOUT WITH SOUR CREAM MASH

We used diced lamb cut from a trimmed leg in this recipe. While we stirred the mashed potatoes into the ragout here, you can serve them in a separate dish, if you desire.

2 tablespoons vegetable oil
800g diced lamb
3 medium (450g) brown onions
6 cloves garlic, crushed
250g small button mushrooms, halved
2 medium (400g) red capsicums, seeded, chopped
2 tablespoons finely chopped fresh sage leaves
3 1/2 cups (875ml) lamb or beef stock
1 tablespoon tomato paste
1 tablespoon finely chopped fresh parsley

SOUR CREAM MASH

4 medium (800g) potatoes, chopped coarsely
1/2 cup (125ml) sour cream
1 teaspoon freshly ground black pepper

Heat half the oil in large pan; cook lamb, in batches, stirring, until browned.

Halve onions; cut each half into wedges. Heat remaining oil in same pan; add onion, garlic, and mushrooms. Cook, stirring, until onion is browned lightly. Stir in capsicum, sage, stock, paste and lamb. Bring to boil; simmer, covered, for 40 minutes. Uncover; simmer for about 30 minutes or until lamb is tender and sauce thickens. *[Can be made ahead to this stage. Cover; refrigerate overnight.]*

Just before serving, add Sour Cream Mash; stir twice, sprinkle with parsley.

Sour Cream Mash Boil, steam or microwave potatoes until tender; drain. Mash potatoes in large bowl with sour cream and pepper.

SERVES 4 TO 6

Opposite above Lamb rendang
Left No-fuss cassoulet
Above Lamb ragout with sour cream mash

LANCASHIRE HOTPOT

6 lamb kidneys
2 teaspoons salt
2 tablespoons vegetable oil
1kg diced lamb
2 medium (240g) carrots, sliced
1 large (500g) leek, sliced
150g button mushrooms, halved
2 tablespoons plain flour

1 tablespoon Worcestershire sauce
1½ cups (370ml) lamb or
    beef stock
1 cup (250ml) water
2 teaspoons finely chopped
    fresh thyme
1 teaspoon freshly ground
    black pepper
4 medium (800g) potatoes, sliced
30g butter

Remove skin and fat from kidneys; cover with cold water in large bowl, stir in salt. Cover; refrigerate overnight.

Drain kidneys; rinse under cold water, drain. Halve kidneys lengthways, remove and discard core of fat; cut remaining kidney into 2cm cubes.

Heat half the oil in large pan; cook lamb, in batches, until browned all over. Place lamb in a deep 3-litre (12-cup) ovenproof dish. Cook kidney in same pan, stirring, until browned all over; add to lamb in dish.

Heat remaining oil in same pan; cook carrot, leek and mushrooms, stirring, until leek is soft. Stir in flour; cook, stirring, until mixture bubbles. Remove from heat; gradually stir in sauce, stock, water, thyme and pepper. Bring to boil; simmer, stirring, for about 5 minutes or until mixture boils and thickens. Combine the vegetable mixture with lamb and kidney mixture in dish; top with potato slices, drizzle with melted butter. *[Can be made ahead to this stage. Cover tightly with plastic wrap; refrigerate overnight.]*

Bake, covered, in moderate oven for 1 hour; uncover, bake about 30 minutes or until top is browned lightly and hotpot cooked through.

SERVES 4 TO 6

RACK OF LAMB WITH CHILLI-ORANGE GLAZE

½ cup (125ml) orange juice
½ cup (125ml) orange marmalade
2 tablespoons mild chilli sauce
2 tablespoons seeded mustard
2 racks of lamb with 6 cutlets each

Combine juice, marmalade, sauce and mustard in small pan. Bring to boil; remove from heat.

Place lamb in large oiled baking dish; pour over hot glaze. Bake, uncovered, in moderate oven about 40 minutes or until lamb is browned and cooked as desired, spooning glaze over lamb occasionally.

SERVES 4 TO 6

Dish from The Bay Tree Kitchen Shop

Left Lancashire hotpot
Right Rack of lamb with chilli-orange glaze

POT ROAST CALABRESE WITH CREAMED POLENTA

Lamb neck fillet roasts have to be ordered from your butcher; ask that the lamb be tied securely.

2 medium (400g) red capsicums
2 medium (400g) yellow capsicums
1/4 cup (60ml) olive oil
1.5kg lamb neck fillet roasts
2 medium (300g) onions,
   sliced thickly
3 cloves garlic, crushed
400g can tomatoes
1 cup (250ml) dry red wine
2 tablespoons lamb or chicken stock
2 tablespoons tomato paste
1 tablespoon finely chopped
   fresh oregano

CREAMED POLENTA
1.25 litres (5 cups) water
1 1/4 cups (250g) polenta
50g butter
1/2 cup (40g) coarsely grated
   parmesan cheese
3/4 cup (180ml) cream
1/4 cup (60ml) lamb or
   chicken stock

Halve capsicums; remove and discard seeds and membranes, cut each half into 4 equal-size slices.

Heat half the oil in large pan; cook lamb, in batches, until browned lightly. Heat remaining oil in same pan; cook onion, garlic and capsicum, stirring, until onion is soft. Return lamb to pan with the undrained crushed tomatoes and all the remaining ingredients; bring to boil. Simmer, covered, 1 1/2 hours; uncover, simmer 1 hour. Remove lamb from pan, remove and discard string; cover lamb to keep warm. Bring tomato mixture in pan to boil; simmer, uncovered, about 20 minutes or until tomato mixture thickens. Return lamb to pan. *[Can be made ahead to this stage. Cover; refrigerate overnight.]* Serve lamb and tomato mixture with the Creamed Polenta.

Creamed Polenta Bring water to boil in large pan; reduce heat, gradually whisk in polenta. Cook, stirring, over medium heat, 30 minutes. Stir in remaining ingredients until heated through; serve immediately.

SERVES 6

Above left Pot roast Calabrese with creamed polenta
Left Braised lamb drumsticks with lentils
Opposite Shepherd's pie

Baking dish from Accoutrement

BRAISED LAMB DRUMSTICKS WITH LENTILS

Drumsticks are French-trimmed lamb shanks; you'll have to ask your butcher to prepare them for you in advance.

1 tablespoon olive oil
8 lamb drumsticks
1 large (200g) onion, sliced
2 cloves garlic, crushed
2 x 425g cans tomatoes
1/3 cup (80ml) dry red wine
2/3 cup (160ml) water
2 baby (120g) eggplants, sliced
**2 small (180g) green
   zucchini, sliced**
**2 small (180g) yellow
   zucchini, sliced**
1 cup (200g) brown lentils
**1 tablespoon finely chopped
   fresh parsley**

Heat oil in large pan; cook lamb, in batches, until browned all over. Add onion and garlic to same pan; cook, stirring, until onion is soft. Return lamb to pan with undrained crushed tomatoes, wine and water. Bring to boil; simmer, uncovered, 1 1/2 hours or until lamb is tender, stirring occasionally. *[Can be made ahead to this stage. Cover; refrigerate overnight or freeze.]* Add eggplant and zucchini; simmer. covered, 25 minutes.

Meanwhile, cook lentils in large pan of boiling water, uncovered, until just soft; drain. Add lentils to lamb mixture; cook, stirring, about 5 minutes or until mixture is hot and lentils are tender. Just before serving, sprinkle with parsley.

SERVES 4

SHEPHERD'S PIE

1 tablespoon vegetable oil
1kg minced lamb
1 medium (150g) onion, chopped
1 medium (120g) carrot, chopped
2 tablespoons plain flour
1 tablespoon tomato paste
1 tablespoon Worcestershire sauce
1 teaspoon dried thyme
**1 1/2 cups (375ml) lamb or
   beef stock**
20g butter

MASHED POTATO TOPPING
3 large (900g) potatoes, halved
30g butter
1/3 cup (80ml) milk, approximately

Heat half the oil in large pan; cook lamb, stirring, until browned, remove from pan. Heat remaining oil in same pan; cook onion and carrot, stirring, until onion is browned lightly. Return lamb to pan, stir in flour; cook, stirring, until mixture bubbles. Stir in paste, sauce, thyme and stock; bring to boil, stirring, until mixture thickens. Simmer, uncovered, 30 minutes. *[Can be made ahead to this stage. Cover; refrigerate overnight or freeze.]* Spoon into shallow oiled 1.5-litre (6-cup) oven-proof dish. Pipe or spread Mashed Potato Topping over lamb mixture; drizzle with melted butter.

Bake, uncovered, in moderate oven about 30 minutes or until top is browned.

Mashed Potato Topping Boil, steam or microwave potato until tender; drain, push potato through sieve; stir in butter and enough milk until a smooth consistency.

SERVES 4 TO 6

Above Herb and cheese-crumbed rack of lamb
Right Braised lamb with broad beans

HERB AND CHEESE-CRUMBED RACK OF LAMB

2 cups (140g) stale white breadcrumbs
4 cloves garlic, crushed
1/2 cup (20g) finely grated parmesan cheese
1/2 cup finely chopped fresh basil leaves

2 tablespoons finely chopped fresh rosemary
1/2 cup (125ml) olive oil
2 racks of lamb with 6 cutlets each

Blend or process breadcrumbs, garlic, cheese, herbs and oil until pureed. *[Can be made 1 day ahead. Cover; refrigerate.]*

Remove excess fat from lamb; place in large oiled baking dish. Press breadcrumb

BRAISED LAMB WITH BROAD BEANS

You will have to pre-order rolled and tied lamb neck fillets from your butcher.

1.5kg lamb neck fillet roasts
2 tablespoons plain flour
2 tablespoons vegetable oil
1 cup (250ml) dry red wine
1/2 cup (125ml) port
2 tablespoons cranberry sauce
1 tablespoon chopped fresh thyme
15 (600g) tiny new potatoes
200g button mushrooms
500g frozen broad beans,
   thawed, peeled

Cut lamb in half widthways; toss lamb in large bowl with flour. Heat oil in large pan; cook lamb, in batches, until browned lightly. Return lamb to pan with wine, port, sauce and thyme. Bring to boil; simmer, covered, 1 1/2 hours. Add whole potatoes and mushrooms then simmer, uncovered, about 1 hour or until potatoes are just tender. *[Can be made ahead to this stage. Cover; refrigerate overnight.]* Add broad beans; simmer, covered, about 5 minutes or until beans are just tender.

SERVES 4 TO 6

mixture onto fatty side of lamb; bake, uncovered, in moderately hot oven about 25 minutes or until browned and cooked as desired.

SERVES 4 TO 6

Soup tureen and bowls from Waterford Wedgwood

Toss lamb in flour, shake off excess. Heat half the oil in large pan; cook lamb, in batches, until browned all over.

Heat remaining oil in same pan; cook onion and garlic, stirring, until onion is soft. Return lamb to pan; add carrot, stock and mustard. Bring to boil; simmer, covered, about 1½ hours or until lamb is tender, stirring occasionally. *[Can be made ahead to this stage. Cover, refrigerate overnight or freeze.]* Add spinach and basil; cook, stirring, until just wilted.

SERVES 4 TO 6

CRUMBED BRAINS WITH BACON AND CRESS

8 sets lamb brains
2 teaspoons salt
1/3 cup (50g) plain flour
4 (320g) bacon rashers
2 tablespoons vegetable oil
1 tablespoon grated lemon rind
1/2 cup (35g) stale breadcrumbs
40g butter
100g trimmed watercress
1/3 cup (80ml) lemon juice
1/3 cup (80ml) olive oil
2 cloves garlic, crushed
1 teaspoon sugar

SCOTCH BROTH

1 tablespoon vegetable oil
4 (500g) lamb neck chops
3 cloves garlic, crushed
2 medium (300g) red
    onions, chopped
2 large (360g) carrots, chopped
3/4 (150g) pearl barley, rinsed
2 bay leaves
1.5 litres (6 cups) lamb or
    vegetable stock
1 medium (350g) leek, sliced
200g (18) seeded prunes, halved
1 litre (4 cups) water
1½ cups (120g) finely
    shredded cabbage

Heat the oil in a large pan; cook lamb, uncovered, until browned both sides. Remove from pan. Add garlic and onion to same pan; cook, stirring, until onion is soft. Add carrot, barley, leaves, stock and lamb. Bring to boil; simmer, uncovered, 30 minutes. Add leek, prunes and water. Bring to boil; simmer, uncovered, about

40 minutes or until lamb is tender. Stir in cabbage; cook about 4 minutes or until cabbage is tender. Remove and discard bay leaves. *[Best if made ahead; cover, refrigerate overnight.]*

SERVES 4

LAMB SHANKS WITH SPINACH AND BASIL

8 lamb shanks
plain flour
2 tablespoons olive oil
2 medium (300g) onions, sliced
2 cloves garlic, crushed
3 large (540g) carrots, chopped
3 cups (750ml) lamb or
    chicken stock
1 tablespoon Dijon mustard
500g spinach, trimmed
1/4 cup finely shredded fresh
    basil leaves

Pan from Accoutrement

Place the sets of brains in a large bowl, cover with cold water; stir in salt. Cover, refrigerate overnight.

Drain brains; halve each set. Using scissors, carefully remove membranes and veins. Cover brains with cold water in medium pan, bring to boil; simmer, uncovered, for 2 minutes. Drain brains; discard cooking liquid. Pat brains dry with absorbent paper; toss brains in flour.

Remove and discard bacon rind; halve rashers crossways. Grill bacon until crisp both sides; drain on absorbent paper.

Heat vegetable oil in large non-stick pan; cook lemon rind and breadcrumbs, stirring, until browned lightly. Remove from pan.

Heat butter in same pan; cook brains about 5 minutes or until browned all over and cooked through. Serve brains with bacon, breadcrumb mixture, watercress and combined remaining ingredients.

SERVES 8

Opposite Scotch broth
Below Lamb shanks with spinach and basil
Right Crumbed brains with bacon and cress

Stemware and china from The Bay Tree Kitchen Shop

YOGURT-LU KEBAB

*Yogurt-lu kebab is one of the most delectable
of all of the many kinds of Turkish kebabs.
Soak bamboo skewers in water for at least
1 hour to avoid scorching. Lamb round roast
has to be ordered from a butcher but you can
use meat diced from a leg of lamb.*

1.2kg lamb round roast
1/2 cup (125ml) yogurt
2 tablespoons olive oil
2 tablespoons lemon juice
**1 tablespoon chopped
    fresh thyme**
3 cloves garlic, crushed
1 teaspoon cracked black pepper
12 pocket pitta

TOMATO SAUCE
**2 medium (120g) long
    green chillies**
2 large (500g) tomatoes
1 tablespoon olive oil
1 teaspoon white wine vinegar

YOGURT SAUCE
200ml yogurt
1/4 cup (60ml) milk
1 tablespoon lemon juice
1 clove garlic, crushed
1 teaspoon sugar

Cut lamb into 3cm pieces; thread onto
12 bamboo skewers. Place skewers, in
single layer, in shallow dish; cover with
combined yogurt, oil, juice, thyme, garlic
and pepper. Cover; refrigerate overnight,
turning skewers occasionally.

Cook skewers, in batches, on heated
oiled griddle (or grill or barbecue) until
browned all over and cooked as desired.
Serve lamb drizzled with Tomato Sauce
and Yogurt Sauce, accompanied with
warmed pitta.

Tomato Sauce Quarter chillies; remove
and discard seeds and membranes. Roast
chilli under grill or in very hot oven, skin-
side up, until skin blisters and blackens.
Cover chilli in plastic for 5 minutes, peel
away skin. Cut each tomato into 8 wedges;

place on wire rack over baking dish. Bake,
uncovered, in moderately hot oven about
30 minutes or until browned lightly.
Blend or process chilli, tomato, oil and
vinegar until pureed. *[Can be made
ahead; cover, refrigerate overnight.]*

Yogurt Sauce Whisk all ingredients
together in small bowl. *[Can be made
ahead; cover, refrigerate overnight.]*

SERVES 4 TO 6

Above Yogurt-lu kebabs
Right Lamb do piazza with banana
tamarind sambal

LAMB DO PIAZZA WITH BANANA TAMARIND SAMBAL

This traditional Indian curry uses onions as a main ingredient rather than just a flavouring, dividing them in half and cooking each in a different way. On average, 2 large overripe bananas make 1 cup mashed banana.

5 cloves garlic, crushed
2 teaspoons grated fresh ginger
1 teaspoon cardamom seeds
1 teaspoon ground turmeric
1 teaspoon cayenne pepper
2 tablespoons water
5 large (1kg) onions, sliced
1kg diced lamb
1/3 cup (80ml) vegetable oil
1 teaspoon fennel seeds
2 teaspoons fenugreek seeds
3/4 cup (180ml) yogurt
4 small (500g) tomatoes, seeded, diced
2 cups (500ml) lamb or beef stock
2 tablespoons lime juice
1/4 cup finely chopped fresh coriander leaves

BANANA TAMARIND SAMBAL
1 tablespoon tamarind paste
2 teaspoons sugar
1 teaspoon ground cumin
1 cup mashed bananas
1 tablespoon lemon juice
1/4 cup (35g) dried currants

Blend or process the garlic, ginger, cardamom, turmeric, pepper, water and half the onion until pureed; transfer marinade to large bowl. Add lamb; toss to coat with marinade. Cover; refrigerate 3 hours or overnight.

Heat oil in large pan; cook remaining onion until browned lightly. Remove from pan; reserve. Add both seeds to same pan; cook, stirring, 1 minute or until seeds pop. Add the lamb mixture; cook, stirring, until browned all over. Add yogurt, in 4 batches, stirring well between each addition. Add tomatoes and stock, bring to boil; simmer, covered, about 1 hour or until lamb is tender.

Stir in the reserved onions; simmer, uncovered, until heated through. *[Can be made ahead to this stage. Cover; refrigerate overnight or freeze.]*

Just before serving, stir in juice and coriander; serve accompanied by Banana Tamarind Sambal.

Banana Tamarind Sambal Combine all ingredients in small bowl. Cover, refrigerate 30 minutes. *[Can be made 1 day ahead; cover, refrigerate.]*

SERVES 4 TO 6

China from Home & Garden on the Mall

A little saucery

Elevate your next meal into the sphere of the sublime by accompanying the lamb with the most complementary of these.

PASTES AND MARINADES

Marinades can be made 2 days ahead; keep covered, in the refrigerator. Marinated meats, covered tightly, can be frozen.

Sherry, Orange and Mustard Marinade

2 teaspoons grated orange rind
2 tablespoons seeded mustard
2 tablespoons sweet sherry
1/2 cup (125ml) orange juice
1 tablespoon balsamic vinegar
1/4 cup (60ml) light olive oil
1/2 teaspoon cracked black pepper

Blend or process all ingredients until combined; pour over lamb cut of choice in large bowl. Cover; refrigerate 3 hours or overnight.

MAKES ABOUT 3/4 CUP (180ml)

Sun-Dried Capsicum, Lime and Balsamic Marinade

1/3 cup (50g) drained sun-dried capsicums, chopped coarsely
1 tablespoon finely grated lime rind
2 tablespoons lime juice
2 tablespoons olive oil
1 tablespoon balsamic vinegar
1/2 teaspoon sugar

Blend or process all ingredients until combined; pour over lamb cut of choice in large bowl. Cover; refrigerate 3 hours or overnight.

MAKES ABOUT 3/4 CUP (180ml)

Italian Herb Marinade

2 tablespoons finely chopped fresh basil leaves
2 tablespoons finely chopped fresh oregano
2 tablespoons finely chopped fresh flat-leaf parsley
2 teaspoons sambal oelek
2 teaspoons finely grated lemon rind
4 cloves garlic, crushed
1/4 cup (60ml) olive oil

Combine all ingredients in small jug; pour over lamb cut of choice in large bowl. Cover; refrigerate 3 hours or overnight.

MAKES ABOUT 1/2 CUP (125ml)

Lemon, Coriander and Yogurt Marinade

200ml yogurt
2 cloves garlic, crushed
1/4 cup (60ml) lemon juice
2 tablespoons finely chopped fresh coriander leaves

Combine all ingredients in small jug; pour over lamb cut of choice in large bowl. Cover; refrigerate 3 hours or overnight.

MAKES ABOUT 1 CUP (250ml)

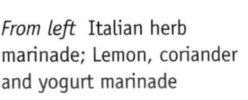

From left Italian herb marinade; Lemon, coriander and yogurt marinade

Teriyaki Marinade

1/2 cup (125ml) teriyaki sauce
2 cloves garlic, crushed
2 teaspoons grated fresh ginger
1 tablespoon mirin

Blend or process all ingredients until combined; pour over lamb cut of choice in large bowl. Cover; refrigerate 3 hours or overnight.

MAKES ABOUT 2/3 CUP (160ml)

Plum Marinade

2 tablespoons white vinegar
1/2 teaspoon nutmeg
1 teaspoon salt
2 cloves garlic, crushed
2 tablespoons brown sugar
1/4 cup (60ml) plum jam
1/3 cup (80ml) tomato sauce
1 tablespoon soy sauce
1 tablespoon hot chilli sauce

Combine all ingredients in small jug; pour over lamb cut of choice in large bowl. Cover; refrigerate 3 hours or overnight.

MAKES ABOUT 1 CUP (250ml)

Spicy Vindaloo Paste

1 tablespoon ground cumin
3 teaspoons chilli powder
3 teaspoons black mustard seeds
1 teaspoon ground cinnamon
1 teaspoon salt
2 1/2 teaspoons cracked black pepper
2 teaspoons ground turmeric
1/2 teaspoon ground cardamom
3 teaspoons garam masala
4 cloves garlic, crushed
1 teaspoon sugar
1 tablespoon finely grated
**   fresh ginger**
1/3 cup (80ml) brown vinegar

Combine all ingredients in small bowl; stand 30 minutes before spreading over lamb cut of choice in large bowl. Cover; refrigerate 3 hours or overnight.

MAKES ABOUT 1/2 CUP (125ml)

Left Vindaloo paste, homemade from turmeric, cumin, chilli powder, garam masala, cracked black pepper and ground cardamom

SAUCES, SALSAS AND DRESSINGS

Fiery Sweet Tomato Chilli Sauce

When chopping unseeded chillies, wear kitchen gloves to avoid burning your skin — and don't rub your eyes or scratch your face while wearing these gloves! This delicious sauce will keep for a few months if packed in hot sterilised jars and sealed when cold.

- 1 tablespoon vegetable oil
- 1 large (200g) onion, chopped
- 4 cloves garlic, crushed
- 1/2 cup (50g) fresh bird's-eye chillies, chopped finely
- 4 large (1kg) tomatoes, peeled and chopped
- 1/2 cup (80g) sultanas
- 1/2 cup (125ml) tomato paste
- 3/4 cup (180ml) white vinegar
- 1 cup (250ml) water
- 1/2 cup (100g) firmly packed brown sugar
- 1/2 cup (110g) caster sugar
- 2 teaspoons salt
- 2 tablespoons finely chopped fresh oregano

Heat oil in medium pan; cook onion, garlic and chilli, stirring, until onion is soft. Add tomatoes and sultanas; cook, stirring, until tomatoes are pulpy. Blend or process hot tomato mixture, in batches, until smooth; return to same pan. Stir in paste, vinegar, water, sugars and salt; bring to boil. Simmer, uncovered, 40 minutes, stirring occasionally. Strain sauce into large bowl; discard the pulp. Return sauce to pan; simmer, uncovered, until sauce thickens, stir in oregano.

MAKES ABOUT 3 CUPS (750ml)

Salsa of Three Capsicums

- 1 small (150g) red capsicum
- 1 small (150g) green capsicum
- 1 small (150g) yellow capsicum
- 1 tablespoon balsamic vinegar
- 1 tablespoon olive oil

Quarter capsicums, remove seeds and membranes. Roast under grill or in very hot oven, skin-side up, until skin blisters and blackens. Cover capsicum pieces in plastic or paper for 5 minutes, peel away skin, chop capsicum finely. Combine capsicum in small bowl with vinegar and oil; stand 30 minutes before serving. *[Best made on day of serving. Cover; refrigerate.]*

MAKES ABOUT 1 1/2 CUPS (375ml)

Horseradish and Basil Sauce

- 200ml yogurt
- 1/3 cup firmly packed fresh basil leaves
- 2 tablespoons horseradish cream
- 1 clove garlic, crushed
- 1/2 teaspoon cracked black pepper

Blend or process all ingredients until sauce is almost smooth. *[Best made on day of serving. Cover; refrigerate.]*

MAKES ABOUT 1 CUP (250ml)

Traditional Mint Sauce

- 1/4 cup finely chopped fresh mint leaves
- 1 tablespoon brown sugar
- 1 teaspoon salt
- 1/4 teaspoon ground black pepper
- 1/4 cup (60ml) boiling water
- 1 cup (250ml) cider vinegar

Combine all ingredients in small bowl; stand 30 minutes before serving. *[Best made on day of serving. Cover; refrigerate.]*

MAKES ABOUT 1 1/4 CUPS (310ml)

Mustard and Green Peppercorn Cream Sauce

- 40g butter
- 1 clove garlic, crushed
- 1 tablespoon plain flour
- 1 1/2 cups (375ml) chicken stock
- 1 tablespoon Dijon mustard
- 1/4 cup (60ml) sour cream
- 3 teaspoons drained green peppercorns

*Above left Fiery sweet tomato chilli sauce
Left Traditional mint sauce*

Heat butter in medium pan; cook garlic, stirring, until soft. Add flour; cook, stirring, until mixture bubbles. Gradually stir in stock and mustard; stir until mixture boils and thickens. Stir in the cream and green peppercorns; simmer, uncovered, until heated through. *[Best made on day of serving. Cover; refrigerate.]*

MAKES ABOUT 1 1/2 CUPS (375ml)

Roasted Capsicum and Onion Dressing

- 1 medium (200g) red capsicum
- 20g butter
- 1 medium (150g) onion, chopped
- 2 cloves garlic, crushed
- 1/2 cup (125ml) olive oil
- 1 tablespoon white wine vinegar
- 2 teaspoons Dijon mustard
- 1/2 teaspoon cracked black pepper
- 1 teaspoon sugar

Quarter capsicum, remove seeds and membranes. Roast under grill or in very hot oven, skin-side up, until skin blisters and blackens. Cover capsicum pieces in plastic or paper for 5 minutes, peel away skin; chop capsicum roughly.

Heat butter in small pan; cook onion and garlic, stirring, until onion is soft. Blend or process capsicum and onion mixture with oil, vinegar, mustard, pepper and sugar until dressing is almost smooth. *[Best made on day of serving. Cover; refrigerate.]*

MAKES ABOUT 1 1/2 CUPS (375ml)

RELISHES, JAMS AND CHUTNEYS

Can be made up to 3 days ahead; keep, covered tightly, in the refrigerator.

Red Onion Marmalade

- 80g butter
- 1 tablespoon olive oil
- 4 large (1.2kg) red onions, chopped coarsely
- 1/3 cup (75g) firmly packed brown sugar
- 2 tablespoons balsamic vinegar

Heat butter and oil in large pan; cook onion, stirring, about 15 minutes or until very soft. Stir in sugar and vinegar; cook, stirring, about 30 minutes or until onion has caramelised.

MAKES ABOUT 2 CUPS (500ml)

Pear, Mint and Green Onion Chutney

1¼ cups firmly packed fresh mint leaves, chopped finely
8 green onions, chopped finely
½ cup (125ml) lime juice
⅓ cup (75g) firmly packed brown sugar
½ teaspoon salt
1 large (330g) pear, chopped finely
2 teaspoons garam masala
1½ tablespoons cider vinegar

Combine 1 cup of the mint and all but 1 tablespoon of the onion in medium pan with remaining ingredients; cook, stirring, until pear is tender and chutney thickens. Remove heat; stir in remaining mint and onion.

MAKES ABOUT 2 CUPS (500ml)

Beer and Onion Relish

2 tablespoons olive oil
2 cloves garlic, crushed
6 large (1.2kg) brown onions, chopped coarsely
2 tablespoons seeded mustard
1½ cups (375ml) lager beer
½ cup (75g) dried currants
½ cup (100g) firmly packed brown sugar
¼ cup (60ml) white wine vinegar
1 teaspoon salt

Heat oil in large pan; add garlic and onion, stirring, about 15 minutes or until onion is very soft. Add mustard; cook, stirring, 1 minute. Stir in remaining ingredients. Bring to boil; simmer, uncovered, about 40 minutes or until mixture thickens, stirring occasionally. Pour hot relish into hot sterilised jars, seal immediately.

MAKES ABOUT 1 LITRE (4 CUPS)

Chilli Jam

1 tablespoon peanut oil
2 cloves garlic, crushed
1 small (100g) red onion, chopped finely
1 tablespoon finely chopped fresh ginger
4 large (1kg) tomatoes, seeded, chopped
¼ cup firmly packed fresh basil leaves, shredded
6 small fresh red chillies, seeded, chopped
¾ cup (180ml) red wine vinegar
¾ cup (180ml) dry sherry
¾ cup (165g) raw sugar

Heat oil in medium pan; cook garlic, onion and ginger, stirring, until onion is soft. Stir in remaining ingredients. Bring to the boil, stirring; simmer, stirring occasionally, about 45 minutes or until jam thickens.

MAKES 1½ CUPS (375ml)

Above Pear, mint and green onion chutney
Right Pumpkin and brandy marmalade

Pumpkin and Brandy Marmalade

500g grated raw butternut pumpkin
1 cup (220g) caster sugar
⅓ cup (80ml) water
2 tablespoons grated orange rind
2 tablespoons grated lemon rind
⅓ cup (80ml) lemon juice
50g butter
2 tablespoons brandy

Combine all ingredients in medium pan. Bring to boil, stirring; simmer, about 45 minutes or until marmalade thickens, stirring occasionally.

MAKES ABOUT 2½ CUPS (625ml)

Cashew, Coriander and Mint Pesto

1¾ cups (275g) raw cashews, toasted
3 bunches (300g) fresh coriander
¼ cup firmly packed fresh mint leaves
¼ cup (60ml) lime juice
⅔ cup (160ml) olive oil

Blend or process cashews, coriander, mint and juice until well combined. With motor operating, gradually pour in oil; process until thick. [*Best made on day of serving. Cover; refrigerate.*]

MAKES ABOUT 2¼ CUPS (560ml)

BUTTERS

Each butter recipe is enough to accompany a lamb dish serving 4 to 6.

Wasabi Butter

125g butter, softened
1½ tablespoons wasabi paste
½ teaspoon honey

Combine all ingredients in small bowl. Cover tightly; refrigerate until firm. *[Can be made ahead. Cover; refrigerate up to 3 days or freeze.]*

Pizza Butter

100g salami, chopped
2 green onions, chopped coarsely
1 tablespoon coarsely chopped fresh oregano
1 clove garlic, crushed
1 tablespoon chopped drained sun-dried tomatoes
125g butter, softened

Blend or process all ingredients until combined. Cover tightly; refrigerate until firm. *[Can be made ahead. Cover; refrigerate up to 3 days or freeze.]*

Chilli, Lime and Red Capsicum Butter

½ small (75g) red capsicum
125g butter, softened
1 tablespoon lime juice
2 tablespoons coarsely chopped fresh coriander leaves
1 small fresh red chilli, halved, seeded
2 teaspoons seeded mustard
1 tablespoon sweet chilli sauce
1 clove garlic, crushed

Roast capsicum under grill or in very hot oven, skin-side up, until skin blisters and blackens. Cover capsicum in plastic or paper for 5 minutes; peel away skin, cut capsicum into small dice.

Blend or process remaining ingredients until combined; place in small bowl, stir in capsicum. Cover tightly; refrigerate until firm. *[Can be made ahead. Cover; refrigerate up to 3 days or freeze.]*

Left Chilli, lime and red capsicum butter on grilled lamb chops
Clockwise from top Pizza butter; Lemon, olive and garlic butter; Wasabi butter; Fresh mint butter

Roasted Garlic Butter

1 medium (70g) bulb garlic
¼ cup (60ml) olive oil
125g butter, softened
2 teaspoons drained baby capers

Place garlic on oven tray, brush with a little of the oil; bake, uncovered, in moderately hot oven about 40 minutes or until garlic softens. Cool; cut bulb in half, squeeze pulp into small bowl, mash with a fork until smooth. Beat butter in small bowl until light and creamy; stir in garlic, remaining oil and capers. Cover tightly; refrigerate until firm. *[Can be made ahead. Cover; refrigerate up to 3 days or freeze.]*

Fresh Mint Butter

125g butter, softened
⅓ cup firmly packed fresh mint leaves
1 clove garlic
1 tablespoon mint jelly

Blend or process all ingredients until combined; season with salt and pepper to taste, if desired. Cover tightly; refrigerate until firm. *[Can be made ahead. Cover; refrigerate up to 3 days or freeze.]*

Chilli and Ginger Butter

1 red chilli, seeded, chopped
1 tablespoon finely grated fresh ginger
2 tablespoons chopped fresh coriander leaves
125g butter, softened

Blend or process all ingredients until combined. Cover tightly; refrigerate until firm. *[Can be made ahead. Cover; refrigerate up to 3 days or freeze.]*

Three-Cheese Butter

¼ cup (50g) fetta cheese
¼ cup (20g) coarsely grated parmesan cheese
¼ cup (30g) coarsely grated cheddar cheese
125g butter, softened
2 tablespoons finely chopped fresh chives

Blend or process all ingredients until combined. Cover tightly; refrigerate until firm. *[Can be made ahead. Cover; refrigerate up to 3 days or freeze.]*

Lemon and Poppy Seed Butter

125g butter, softened
2 cloves garlic, crushed
1 tablespoon finely grated lemon rind
¼ teaspoon sweet paprika
1 teaspoon English mustard
2 teaspoons poppy seeds

Combine all ingredients in small bowl. Cover tightly; refrigerate until firm. *[Can be made ahead. Cover; refrigerate up to 3 days or freeze.]*

Lemon, Olive and Garlic Butter

1 small (50g) bulb garlic
125g butter, softened
1 cup (120g) seeded black olives
2 teaspoons grated lemon rind
1 tablespoon lemon juice

Place garlic on oven tray, brush with a little oil; bake, uncovered, in moderately hot oven about 50 minutes or until garlic softens. Cool; cut bulb in half, squeeze pulp into blender or processor. Blend with remaining ingredients until combined; season with salt and pepper to taste, if desired. Cover tightly; refrigerate until firm. *[Can be made ahead. Cover; refrigerate up to 3 days or freeze.]*

The lowdown on lamb

A practical and informative compendium of indispensable tips and helpful suggestions on all aspects of lamb preparation, hygiene, refrigeration, freezing and cooking methods.

Purchasing and storing

When shopping, take along an insulated bag for chilled and frozen meat products, and purchase these items last.

Once home, place all chilled and frozen food in your refrigerator or freezer immediately.

Allow 125g to 150g (about 5oz) of boneless meat per person.

Meat should be a bright, clear colour and have a fresh appearance and smell.

Select lean meat; whatever fat there is should be pale cream in colour.

Meat should be kept as dry as possible and never sit in its own juice. Cold air should be able to circulate freely around the piece of meat.

The more cutting and preparation the meat has been subjected to, the shorter the storage time. This is why storage time for mince (ground meat) is less than roasts or chops.

If meat is used within 2 days, it can be left in its original wrapping.

Meat that has been kept in the refrigerator for 2 to 3 days will be more tender than meat cooked on the day of purchase. This is due to natural enzymes softening the muscle fibre.

To maximise freshness, meat should be refrigerated, in a single layer, in a container covered loosely with foil.

Hygiene

Careful attention to hygiene when handling meat is essential. Most cases of food poisoning result from food being unrefrigerated. The longer food stands at room temperature, the greater the chance of food poisoning.

Wash hands and utensils thoroughly before and after handling meat.

Never handle cooked and uncooked meats together: don't cut them with the same utensils or on the same board.

Store cooked meat above raw meat so there's no chance that juices can drip onto cooked meat.

Defrost frozen meat in the lower part of the refrigerator before cooking: never defrost it at room temperature.

Refrigerate leftover cooked meat as soon as possible.

Refrigeration time for meat

Mince *(ground meat)* and sausages	2 days
Diced meat	2 to 3 days
Chops and cutlets	2 to 3 days
Roasting joints *(with bone in)*	3 to 4 days
Roasting joints *(boned and rolled)*	2 to 3 days

Freezer hints

Meat should be sealed tightly to protect it from freezer burn, dehydration and oxidation of fat.

Set your freezer at -18°C (0°F) or lower.

When freezing chops or cutlets, pack them individually in plastic wrap then in plastic freezer bags, expelling as much air as possible.

Defrost frozen meat in the refrigerator or on defrost setting in a microwave oven.

Do not thaw meat at room temperature or in hot water.

Don't freeze too much at once; smaller batches freeze far more rapidly.

Make sure there is plenty of space in the freezer. Cold air needs to circulate freely around the food so that it freezes quickly.

Mince (ground meat) has a greater surface area, so cook it as soon as possible after defrosting.

PREPARING MEAT TO BE FROZEN

Each package should carry a label showing name of cut, weight or amount and date of packaging.

Meat purchased on a styrofoam tray should be repacked before freezing, discarding styrofoam tray.

Air should be expelled either by pressing out when wrapping or with the aid of a pump. Twist, then seal bags with a strip of masking tape.

Cutting meat into individual portions, strips or cubes before freezing will save time in meal preparation.

Weigh meal-sized portions and place in plastic bags, making sure to fill all corners with meat.

Make packages as flat as possible so that the meat will defrost more rapidly when needed.

Frozen meat storage times
(at -18°C/ 0°F)

Lamb joint *(bone in)*	6 months
Lamb joint *(boned & rolled)*	4 months
Chops, cutlets, etc	4 months

Casseroles and curries

Seal meat in a preheated pan over high heat in small batches to lock in flavoursome juices and develop colour.

Once liquid is added, allow the casserole to return to the boil, then immediately reduce heat. Cover and simmer until tender, stirring occasionally to prevent sticking.

Don't allow a casserole or curry to boil rapidly because doing so will toughen the meat considerably.

A pressure cooker is a great help in cooking casseroles as it can reduce cooking time by about a third.

Stir-fries

Cut meat into thin strips across the grain. This shortens the fibre, making the pieces more tender.

Have the wok or pan well heated: searing the meat seals in the juices and makes it cook more quickly. Too low a temperature stews meat in its own juices and toughens it.

To maintain a consistently high temperature, stir-fry meat in a number of small batches.

If stir-frying marinated meat, thoroughly drain off the marinade before cooking meat. Return any reserved marinade to wok at the end of cooking time, and bring to the boil.

Pan-fries, barbecues and grills

Have pan, barbecue or grill well heated to ensure meat is sealed. Meat should sizzle immediately when it touches the base of the pan or barbecue to avoid it stewing and becoming tough.

When pan-frying and barbecuing, seal meat on both sides. Beads of juice appearing on the uncooked side indicate the meat is ready to turn. If meat is turned too soon or too often, it becomes dry and tough.

Rare meat needs only to be well sealed. To avoid charring if cooking further, reduce heat after the meat is sealed.

Do not cut into meat to see if cooked. Press surface with tongs: cooked meat will offer some resistance and spring back. It is important to rest the meat a little after cooking to allow the juices to settle. Cutting the meat too soon will allow juices to escape.

If using marinades, those containing honey or other sugary ingredients burn easily so it may be necessary to reduce the heat immediately after sealing.

Roasts

Meat can be elevated over a roasting pan, either on a rack or over a bed of vegetables. Using the vegetables also adds flavour to the meat juices that collect in the pan.

The roast should be allowed to rest for 10 to 15 minutes before carving, enabling juices to settle into the meat.

When carving, slice across the grain. This shortens the fibre, making the slices more tender.

Weigh raw meat so you can accurately calculate the cooking time.

For accuracy, use a meat thermometer. Calculate the cooking time then insert the thermometer into the thickest part of the meat.

Internal temperatures:
Rare = 60°C/140°F
Medium = 70°C/160°F
Well done = 75°C/170°F

Not all lamb cuts are calculated the same way or require the same oven temperature due to variation in size.

For small cuts such as neck fillet roast and eye of loin, roast at 220°C/450°F.

- *allow 9 to 10 minutes per 100g for medium*
- *allow 11 to 12 minutes per 100g for well done*

Lamb rack and crown roast require a total 45 to 55 minutes (medium to well done) regardless of weight.

All other cuts should be roasted at 180°C/350°F.

- *allow 20 to 25 minutes per 500g for rare*
- *allow 25 to 30 minutes per 500g for medium*
- *allow 30 to 35 minutes per 500g for well done*

LO

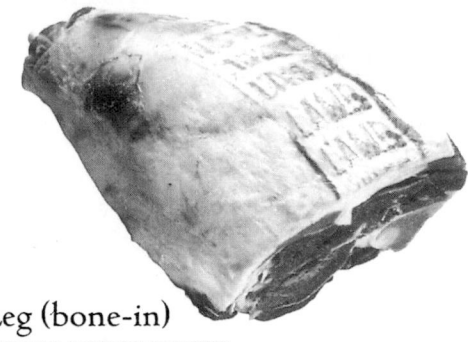

Leg (bone-in)

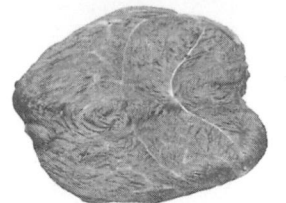

Trim Lamb Schnitzel
(round or topside)

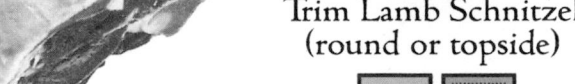

Mince

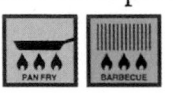

Cutlet

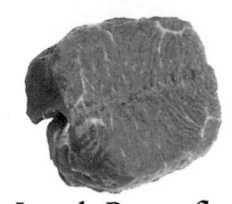

Trim Lamb Butterfly Steak

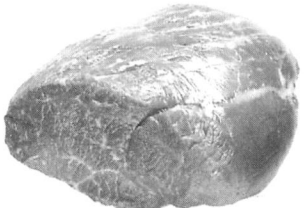

Trim Lamb Mini Roast
(round or topside)

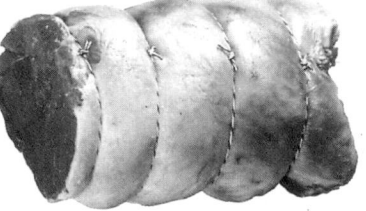

Leg (tunnel-boned)

Trim Lamb E

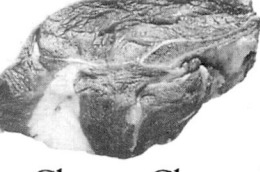

Loin Chop

Trim Lamb Strips

Trim Lamb Steak
(round or topside)

Chump Chop

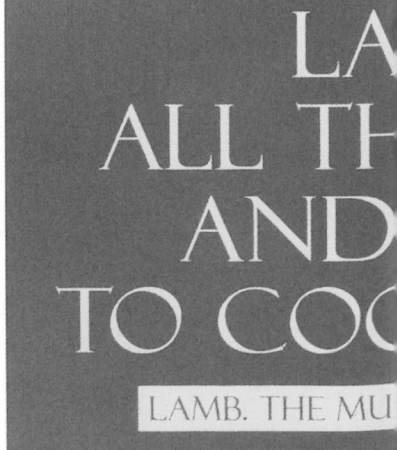

Diced Trim Lamb
(for kebabs)

Easy Carve Leg

FOREQUARTER

Loin (boned and rolled)

Rack of Lamb/
Crown Roast

Loin

Trim Lamb Fillet

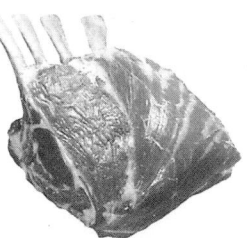

Four Rib Roast

Forequarter Chop

Lamb Drumstick

Party Rack

Party Ribs

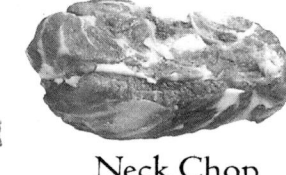

Lamb Shank

Diced (forequarter)

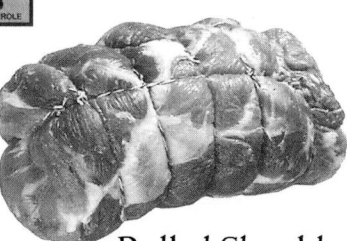

Neck Chop

Rolled Shoulder

Neck Fillet Roast

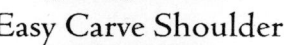

Easy Carve Shoulder

Best Neck Chop

GLOSSARY

BACON RASHERS also known as slices of bacon; made from pork side, cured and smoked. **Streaky bacon** is the fatty end of a bacon rasher (slice), without the lean (eye) meat.

BAKE BLIND cooking term describing a pie shell or pastry case that is baked before filling is added. To **bake blind,** ease pastry into required pan or dish, place pan on oven tray; cover pastry with baking paper, fill with dried rice or "baking beans" (also called "pie weights"). Bake in moderately hot oven 10 minutes, remove paper, beans, etc; bake for a further 10 minutes or until browned lightly. Cool cooked shell or case before adding filling.

BARBECUE SAUCE a spicy, tomato-based sauce used to marinade and baste, or as an accompaniment for meats.

BEANS
Black also called **turtle** beans or **black kidney** beans, these earthy tasting dried beans are not related to Chinese black beans (which are in fact fermented soy beans). Used in Mexican, South American and Caribbean cooking, especially soups and stews.
Broad also known as **fava** beans, these are available fresh, canned and frozen. Fresh broad beans are best when peeled twice, discarding both the outer, long, green pod and the sandy-green, tough inner shell).
Haricot small, dried white bean similar in appearance and flavour to other *Phaseolus vulgaris*, including **great northern**, **navy** and **cannellini** beans.
Mexican-style baked a canned mixture of kidney, haricot or pinto beans cooked with tomato, peppers, onion, garlic and various spices.

BLACK BEAN SAUCE a Chinese sauce made from fermented soy beans, spices, water and wheat flour.

BREADCRUMBS
Packaged fine-textured, crunchy white breadcrumbs.
Stale one- or two-day-old bread crumbed by grating, blending or processing.

BRUISE a kitchen technique where the flat side of a chef's knife is pressed firmly down on certain herbs or spices, such as lemon grass or cardamom, to help release the aroma or taste.

BUCKWHEAT NOODLES also known as **soba**, there are many varieties made of buckwheat and varying proportions of wheat flour — and, sometimes, flavourings such as green tea, spices, etc.

BURGHUL also known as bulghur wheat; hulled, steamed wheat kernels that, once dried, are crushed into various size grains. Used in Middle-Eastern dishes such as kibbeh and tabouleh.

CAJUN SEASONING used to give an authentic Deep South spicy flavour to food, this packaged blend of assorted herbs and spices can include paprika, basil, onion, fennel, thyme, cayenne and tarragon.

CAPERS the grey-green buds of a warm climate (usually Mediterranean) shrub sold either dried and salted, or pickled in a vinegar brine; used to add piquancy to sauces and dressings.

CAPSICUM also known as bell pepper or, simply, pepper. Seeds and membranes should be discarded before use.

CARDAMOM native to India and used extensively in its cuisine; can be purchased in pod, seed or ground form. Has a distinctive aromatic, sweetly rich flavour and is one of the world's most expensive spices.

CHEESE
Bocconcini small rounds of fresh "baby" mozzarella, a delicate, semi-soft, white cheese traditionally made in Italy from buffalo milk. Spoils rapidly so must be kept under refrigeration, in brine, for 1 or 2 days at most.
Cheddar the most common cow milk "tasty" cheese; should be aged, hard and have a pronounced bite.
Fetta Greek in origin, this crumbly goat or

Mexican-style baked beans

sheep milk cheese has a sharp, salty and full-flavoured taste.
Haloumi a firm, creamy-hued sheep milk cheese matured in brine; somewhat like a minty, salty fetta in flavour.
Parmesan a sharp-tasting, dry, hard cheese, made from skim or part-skim milk and aged for at least a year before being sold. The best quality is Parmigiano Reggiano, from Italy, aged for a minimum of three years.
Pizza cheese a commercial blend of varying proportions of processed grated cheddar, mozzarella and parmesan.
Romano a straw-coloured, good-grating, hard cheese with a grainy texture and sharp, tangy flavour, made from a combination of cow and either goat or sheep milk.

CHERMOULLA a piquant Moroccan mixture of fresh and ground spices including coriander, cumin and paprika. This paste may be covered with a thin layer of olive oil to preserve it.

CHICKPEAS also called garbanzos, hummus or channa; an irregularly round, sandy-coloured legume used extensively in Mediterranean, Hispanic and Latin cooking.

CHILLIES also known as hot peppers or chiles; fiery pods belonging to the Capsicum genus, available in many different types and sizes. Use rubber gloves when seeding and chopping fresh chilli to avoid burning your skin; remove seeds and membranes to lessen the heat level. When

haricot beans

black (turtle) beans

chickpeas

cannellini beans

broad beans

fresh chillies are sold dried, they are named differently. For example, fresh jalapeño, cayenne, poblano and chilaca chillies are called chipotle, de arbo, ancho and pasilla, respectively, when dried. Each type has its own flavour and degree of heat; experiment to find which ones you prefer.

Green, Long also known as Thai green; a fresh chilli.

Powder any chilli dried and ground can be blended into chilli powder; Asian varieties are, as a rule, usually the hottest. While the taste will not be exactly the same, you can substitute chilli powder for fresh chillies — but use caution as the degree of heat varies enormously. As a rule, $1/2$ teaspoon chilli powder is the equivalent of 1 medium fresh chopped chilli.

Sauce there are a myriad bottled chilli sauces available, from the hot Chinese variety, made from bird's-eye chillies, salt and vinegar, to the sweet, mild Thai version containing garlic, vinegar and sugar as well as chilli.

CLOVE dried flower buds from a tropical evergreen tree; used whole or in ground form.

COCONUT
Cream available in cans; made from coconut and water.
Desiccated unsweetened, concentrated, dried and shredded coconut.
Flaked dried and flaked coconut flesh.
Freshly grated can be grated from a fresh coconut or purchased, frozen, in packets.
Milk pure, unsweetened coconut milk, available in cans and tetra packs.
Shredded thin strips of dried coconut flesh.

CORIANDER also known as cilantro or Chinese parsley; bright-green leaf with a distinctive pungent flavour. Often stirred into a dish just before serving for flavour impact. The herb's **seeds** are also dried and used, both whole and **ground**, in Indian and Middle-Eastern cooking.

CORNFLOUR (cornstarch); used to thicken sauces, soups, etc, and mixed with flour to give cakes a finer texture.

COUSCOUS a fine, grain-like cereal product, originally from North Africa; made from semolina rolled into balls.

CRACKED WHEAT whole wheat berries broken during milling into a cereal product of varying degrees of coarseness; used in breadmaking.

CRANBERRY SAUCE available canned and bottled; made of cooked cranberries in a sugar syrup, its sweet-sour flavour goes well with roast poultry and meats.

CREAM
Fresh (minimum fat content 35%): also known as pure cream or pouring cream; has no added thickeners.
Sour (minimum fat content 35%): a thick, commercially cultured soured cream.

CURRY
Leaves shiny bright-green, sharp-ended leaves used, fresh or dried, in cooking, especially in Indian and Southeast Asian cooking.
Paste, Green consisting of red onion, green chilli, soy bean oil, garlic, galangal, lemon grass, shrimp paste, citrus peel and coriander seeds.
Paste, Red consisting of chilli, onion, garlic, oil, lemon rind, shrimp paste, cumin, paprika, turmeric and pepper.
Pastes some recipes in this book call for commercially prepared pastes of various strength and flavours, ranging from the bright-red Tandoori, mild Tikka and medium Madras to the fiery Vindaloo. Use whatever suits your spice-level tolerance best.
Powder a blend of ground, powdered spices used for convenience when making Indian food. Can consist of some or all of the following in varying proportions: dried chilli, cinnamon, coriander, cumin, fennel, fenugreek, mace, cardamom and turmeric.

DRUMSTICKS, LAMB French-trimmed lamb shanks.

EGGPLANT also known as aubergine.

EGGS if recipes call for raw or barely cooked eggs, be careful if there is a salmonella problem in your area.

poblano 5/10

chilaca 2/10

Degree of heat, on a scale of 1 (mildest) to 10 (hottest)

Inca gold 7/10

green habanero 8/10

green jalapeño 4/10

bird's-eye 9/10

orange habanero 10/10

red habanero 8/10

red jalapeño 3/10

Thai green 6/10

EN CROUTE cooking term that translates literally as "crust" but is broadly used, describing pastry cases, deep-fried bread bases for meat pieces or for pastry-wrapped pieces of meat cooked by baking.

FENNEL also known as finocchio or anise; word used for both the root vegetable and the dried whole or ground licorice-tasting seed.

FILLO PASTRY also known as phyllo; tissue-thin pastry sheets purchased chilled or frozen that are easy to work with and very versatile, lending themselves to both sweet and savoury dishes.

FISH SAUCE also called nam pla or nuoc nam; made from pulverised, salted, fermented fish, most often anchovies. Has a pungent smell and strong taste; use sparingly. There are many different fish sauces on the market, and the intensity of flavour varies with each one.

FIVE-SPICE POWDER a fragrant mixture of ground cinnamon, cloves, star anise, Sichuan peppercorns and fennel seeds.

FREEKEH Roasted green (young) wheat, sold both whole and cracked; known as frik across North Africa, firik in Turkey, and freekah in Syria and Lebanon. A nutritious and vitamin-rich grain eaten in place of rice and other grains or cereals; 1 cup of dry freekeh makes 3 cups cooked.

GALANGAL also known as **laos**; a member of the ginger family, this dried root is used whole or ground. Has a piquant, peppery flavour.

GARAM MASALA a powdered blend of spices, originally from North India, made up of cardamom, cinnamon, clove, coriander and cumin. Sometimes chilli is added, making a hot variation.

GHEE clarified butter; with the milk solids removed, this fat can be heated to a high temperature without burning.

GINGER
Fresh also known as green or root ginger; the thick gnarled root of a tropical plant. Can be kept, peeled, covered with dry sherry in a jar and refrigerated, or frozen, airtight.
Ground also known as powdered ginger; used as a flavouring in cakes, pies and puddings but cannot be substituted for fresh ginger.

GLACE FIGS also known as candied figs; dried figs preserved in a sugar syrup.

GREEN PEPPERCORNS soft, unripe berry of the pepper plant usually sold packed in brine (occasionally found dried, packed in salt). Distinctive fresh taste that goes well with mustard or cream sauces.

HOISIN SAUCE a thick, sweet and spicy Chinese paste made from salted fermented soy beans, onions and garlic; used as a marinade or baste, or to accent stir-fries and barbecued or roasted foods.

HOKKIEN NOODLES also known as **stir-fry noodles**; fresh wheat flour noodles resembling thick, yellow-brown spaghetti that don't require pre-cooking before being used.

HORSERADISH CREAM a creamy prepared paste of grated horseradish, vinegar, oil and sugar usually served as a condiment.

KAFFIR LIME LEAVES aromatic leaves of a small citrus tree bearing a wrinkled-skinned, yellow-green fruit; originally grown in South Africa and Southeast Asia. Used fresh or dried, whole or torn, in many Asian dishes.

KITCHEN STRING when a recipe calls for a cut of meat to be tied, make sure that you use string constructed of an untreated natural material specifically for use in cooking; synthetic string will melt over heat or in the oven.

KUMARA Polynesian name of the deliciously adaptable orange-fleshed sweet potato which is often incorrectly referred to as a yam.

MADEIRA a rich, dark dessert wine having intense fruit flavour, named after the Portuguese island where it originated. Also a good cooking wine, both for sweet and savoury dishes.

MAPLE SYRUP distilled sap of the maple tree. Maple-flavoured syrup (pancake syrup) is made from cane sugar and artificial maple flavouring and is not an adequate substitute for the real thing.

MINCED (LAMB) also known as ground. If you mince a leg or shoulder at home, trim it of as much fat as possible.

MINT a tangy aromatic herb available fresh or dried.
Jelly a sweetened gelatinous condiment flavoured with mint flakes, salt and various spices; usually served with roast lamb.

MIRIN a sweet, low-alcohol rice wine use in Japanese cooking; not the same as the rice wine **sake** which is neither sweetened nor flavoured.

MIXED SPICE a blend of ground spices usually consisting of cinnamon, allspice and nutmeg.

mint jelly

MUSTARD
Dijon a pale camel-brown, distinctively flavoured, fairly mild French mustard.
Mild English toned-down variation of traditional hot English mustard.
Powder finely ground white (yellow) mustard seeds.
Seeded also known as wholegrain. A course-grain mustard made of crushed mustard seeds in a Dijon-style mustard, often flavoured with herbs or green peppercorns.

NUTS
Pine also known as pignoli; small, cream-coloured kernels obtained from the cones of certain pine trees.
Pistachio pale-green, delicate tasting nut found inside a hard, off-white shell. To peel, soak shelled nuts in boiling water for about 5 minutes; drain, then pat dry with absorbent paper. Rub skins with cloth to peel.

redcurrant jelly

OIL
Macadamia a mono-unsaturated oil extracted from macadamia nuts.
Olive mono-unsaturated; pressed from tree-ripened olives. Good for everyday cooking and as an ingredient.
Extra Light or **Light Olive Oil** describes the mild flavour of the oil and has nothing to do with fat levels.
Peanut pressed from ground peanuts; the most commonly used oil in stir-frying because of its high smoke point.
Sesame made from roasted, crushed white sesame seeds; a flavouring rather than a cooking medium.
Vegetable any of a number of oils sourced from plants rather than animal fats.

OLIVE PASTE seeded and crushed olives blended with additional olive oil, salt, vinegar and herbs; used both as a condiment eaten on its own and an ingredient in sauces and dressings.

OYSTER SAUCE Asian in origin, this rich, dark-brown sauce is made from oysters and their brine, and soy sauce, then thickened with starches.

PANCETTA an Italian salt-cured pork roll, usually cut from the belly; used, chopped, in cooked dishes to add flavours. Bacon can be substituted.

PAPRIKA ground, dried red capsicum (bell pepper), available in sweet and hot versions; if available, the Spanish hot "pimenton" is among the best.

PATE, GREEN PEPPERCORN commercially or home-made cooked meat paste (usually pureed liver) flavoured with softened green peppercorns.

PENNE translates literally as "quills"; ridged macaroni cut diagonally into short lengths.

PEPITAS dried and hulled pumpkin seeds, often sold roasted; good in muesli, salads or as a snack.

PIDE (Turkish bread) long (about 45cm) flat loaves or individual rounds; made from wheat flour and sprinkled with sesame or black onion seeds.

PILAU (also spelled **Pilao**, **Pilav** or **Pilaf**) an Eastern Mediterranean-through-to-India rice- or wheat-based dish where the particular grain or cereal product is stirred in hot oil or butter before being cooked in stock with dried fruits, nuts or aromatics.

PITTA also known as pita, or Lebanese bread or pocket bread; a Middle-Eastern, wheat-flour bread, usually sold pre-packaged in large, flat pieces easily separated into 2 paper-thin rounds. Comes in smaller, thicker pieces as well, commonly called **Pocket Pitta**.

PIZZA BASE commercially packaged pre-cooked wheat-flour round bases, sold in supermarkets in a variety of sizes, ready to be topped and baked by the home cook.

POLENTA a flour-like cereal made from ground corn (maize); similar to cornmeal but coarser and darker in colour; also the name given to the dish made from it.

POMEGRANATE POWDER also known as anardana or anardhath; made from dried and ground seeds of the astringent, wild, bright-red pomegranate. Used in Middle-Eastern meat dishes and South Indian vegetarian cooking.

PORT a sweet, rich, fortified wine which originated in Portugal; various types include Tawny, Ruby and Vintage.

POTATO, TINY NEW also known as baby potatoes or **chats**; these can be any variety of potato, harvested when young enough to retain a waxy appearance and paper-thin skin.

Dinosaur Designs

egg tomato

tomato puree

cherry tomato

tomato paste

PUFF PASTRY SHEETS also called feuillete; 25cm-square, ready-rolled frozen sheets of puff (multi-layered, light) pastry made from wheat flour, vegetable margarine or butter, salt, food acid and water.

RADICCHIO a member of the chicory family, this common Italian lettuce has burgundy to red to green leaves and can be eaten raw, in salads, grilled or fried.

RAISINS dried sweet grapes, also known as muscatels and sultanas. Can be made from any type of grape.

REDCURRANT JELLY a preserve made from redcurrants, used as a glaze for desserts or meats.

SAFFRON stigma of a member of the crocus family, available in strands or ground form; imparts a yellow-orange colour to food once infused. Quality varies greatly; the best is the most expensive spice in the world. Should be covered tightly and kept in the freezer.

SAMBAL OELEK (also **ulek** or **olek**) Indonesian in origin; a salty paste made from ground chillies, sugar and spices.

SEASONED PEPPER a packaged preparation of combined black pepper, red capsicum (bell pepper) and paprika.

SESAME SEEDS black and white are the most common of the oval seeds harvested from the tropical pant *Sesamum indicum*; however, there are red and brown varieties also. White sesame seeds are ground into a paste called **tahini**. To toast: spread seeds evenly onto oven tray, place in moderate oven for about 5 minutes, or stir in heavy-based pan over heat until golden brown.

SHORTCRUST PASTRY SHEETS non-yeast 25cm-square, ready-rolled frozen sheets of short pie dough (that pastry having a high ratio of fat to flour).

SICHUAN PEPPER (also known as **Chinese peppercorns**) small, red-brown aromatic seeds resembling black peppercorns having a peppery-lemon flavour.

SOY SAUCE made from fermented soy beans. Several variations are available in most supermarkets and Asian food stores, among them are salt-reduced, light, thick, sweet and salty.

STAR ANISE a dried, star-shaped pod, the seeds of which have an astringent, aniseed flavour.

SUMAC a purple-red, astringent spice ground from berries growing on shrubs that flourish wild around the Mediterranean and Mid-East; adds a tart and sour, lemony flavour to grilled meats.

TABASCO SAUCE brand name of an extremely fiery sauce made from vinegar, hot red peppers and salt.

TACO SEASONING MIX a packaged seasoning meant to duplicate a Mexican sauce; made from oregano, cumin, chillies and other spices.

TAMARIND PASTE a thick, purple-black, ready-to-use sweet-sour paste extracted from the pulp of pods from tamarind trees; use as is, with no soaking, stirred into casseroles and stews.

TERIYAKI SAUCE a homemade or commercially made sauce consisting of soy sauce, corn syrup, vinegar, ginger and other spices; it imparts a distinctive glaze when brushed on grilled meats.

TOMATO
Cherry also known as Tiny Tim or Tom Thumb tomatoes, small and round.
Egg also called plum or Roma, these are smallish, oval-shaped tomatoes much used in Italian cooking or salads.
Paste a concentrated tomato puree used to flavour soups, stews, sauces and casseroles.
Puree canned pureed tomatoes (not a concentrate). Use fresh, peeled, pureed tomatoes as a substitute.

TORTILLA thin, round unleavened bread originating in Mexico; can be made at home or purchased frozen, fresh or vacuum-packed. Two kinds are available, one made from wheat flour and the other from corn (maizemeal). The word **tortilla**, when used in Spanish as opposed to Mexican kitchens, is the name for an omelette usually filled with potatoes.

TURMERIC a member of the ginger family; the root, when dried and ground, results in the rich yellow powder which gives Indian dishes their characteristic bright colour. It is intensely pungent in taste but not actually hot.

VINEGAR
Balsamic authentic only from the Italian province of Modena; made from a regional wine of white Trebbiano grapes specially processed then aged in antique wooden casks making it exquisitely piquant.

Brown (malt) made from fermented malt barley and beech shavings.
Cider made from various types of fermented apples.
Raspberry made from fresh raspberries steeped in a white wine vinegar.
Red wine based on fermented red wine.
Rice wine made from fermented rice.
White made from spirit of cane sugar.
White wine made from fermented white wine.

WASABI an Asian green horseradish used to make a sharp and biting paste traditionally served with Japanese raw fish dishes.

YEAST a 7g (1/4oz) sachet of dried yeast (2 teaspoons) is equal to 15g (1/2oz) compressed yeast if substituting one for the other.

YOGURT an unflavoured, full-fat cow milk yogurt has been used in these recipes unless stated otherwise. Besides being eaten on its own, yogurt can be used to tenderise meat and thicken sauces.

ZUCCHINI also known as courgette.

tamarind paste

wasabi

chermoulla

olive paste

INDEX

MAKE YOUR OWN STOCK

Recipes can be made 4 days ahead: store, covered, in refrigerator; or freeze, in smaller quantities. Remove any fat that has risen to the surface after stock has been refrigerated overnight.

Stock is available in cans or tetra packs. If using stock cubes or powder, use 1 teaspoon of stock powder or 1 small cube with 1 cup (250ml) water to give a strong stock. Check salt and fat content of packaged stocks.

Recipes make 2.5 litres (10 cups).

LAMB OR BEEF STOCK

2kg meaty bones
2 medium (300g) onions
2 celery sticks, chopped
2 medium (250g) carrots, chopped
3 bay leaves
2 teaspoons black peppercorns
5 litres (20 cups) water
3 litres (12 cups) water, extra

Place bones and unpeeled chopped onions in baking dish. Bake in hot oven about 1 hour or until bones and onions are well browned. Transfer bones and onions to large pan, add celery, carrots, bay leaves, peppercorns and water; simmer, uncovered, 3 hours. Add extra water, simmer, uncovered, further 1 hour; strain.

FISH STOCK

1.5kg fish bones
3 litres (12 cups) water
1 medium (150g) onion, chopped
2 sticks celery, chopped
2 bay leaves
1 teaspoon black peppercorns

Combine all ingredients in large pan, simmer, uncovered, 20 minutes; strain.

CHICKEN STOCK

2kg chicken bones
2 medium (300g) onions, chopped
2 celery sticks, chopped
2 medium (250g) carrots, chopped
3 bay leaves
2 teaspoons black peppercorns
5 litres (20 cups) water

Combine all ingredients in large pan, simmer, uncovered, 2 hours; strain.

VEGETABLE STOCK

2 large (360g) carrots, chopped
2 large (360g) parsnips, chopped
4 medium (600g) onions, chopped
12 celery sticks, chopped
4 bay leaves
2 teaspoons black peppercorns
6 litres (24 cups) water

Combine all ingredients in large pan, simmer, uncovered, 1½ hours; strain.

FACTS AND FIGURES

Wherever you live, you'll be able to use our recipes with the help of these easy-to-follow conversions. While these conversions are approximate only, the difference between an exact and the approximate conversion of various liquid and dry measures is but minimal and will not affect your cooking results.

DRY MEASURES

Metric	Imperial
15g	$1/2$oz
30g	1oz
60g	2oz
90g	3oz
125g	4oz ($1/4$lb)
155g	5oz
185g	6oz
220g	7oz
250g	8oz ($1/2$lb)
280g	9oz
315g	10oz
345g	11oz
375g	12oz ($3/4$lb)
410g	13oz
440g	14oz
470g	15oz
500g	16oz (1lb)
750g	24oz ($1^1/2$lb)
1kg	32oz (2lb)

LIQUID MEASURES

Metric	Imperial
30ml	1 fluid oz
60ml	2 fluid oz
100ml	3 fluid oz
125ml	4 fluid oz
150ml	5 fluid oz ($1/4$ pint/1 gill)
190ml	6 fluid oz
250ml	8 fluid oz
300ml	10 fluid oz ($1/2$ pint)
500ml	16 fluid oz
600ml	20 fluid oz (1 pint)
1000ml (1 litre)	$1^3/4$ pints

HELPFUL MEASURES

Metric	Imperial
3mm	$1/8$in
6mm	$1/4$in
1cm	$1/2$in
2cm	$3/4$in
2.5cm	1in
5cm	2in
6cm	$2^1/2$in
8cm	3in
10cm	4in
13cm	5in
15cm	6in
18cm	7in
20cm	8in
23cm	9in
25cm	10in
28cm	11in
30cm	12in (1ft)

MEASURING EQUIPMENT

The difference between one country's measuring cups and another's is, at most, within a 2 or 3 teaspoon variance. (For the record, 1 Australian metric measuring cup holds approximately 250ml.) The most accurate way of measuring dry ingredients is to weigh them. When measuring liquids, use a clear glass or plastic jug with the metric markings.

If you would like to purchase The Australian Women's Weekly Test Kitchen's metric measuring cups and spoons (as approved by Standards Australia), turn to page 120 for details and order coupon. You will receive:

- a graduated set of 4 cups for measuring dry ingredients, with sizes marked on the cups.
- a graduated set of 4 spoons for measuring dry and liquid ingredients, with amounts marked on the spoons.
- 1 teaspoon: 5ml
- 1 tablespoon: 20ml.

Note: North America and UK use 15ml tablespoons. All cup and spoon measurements are level.

How To Measure

When using graduated metric measuring cups, shake dry ingredients loosely into the appropriate cup. Do not tap the cup on a bench or tightly pack the ingredients unless directed to do so. Level top of measuring cups and measuring spoons with a knife. When measuring liquids, place a clear glass or plastic jug with metric markings on a flat surface to check accuracy at eye level.

We use large eggs having an average weight of 60g.

OVEN TEMPERATURES

These oven temperatures are only a guide. Always check the manufacturer's manual.

	C° (Celsius)	F° (Fahrenheit)	Gas Mark
Very slow	120	250	1
Slow	150	300	2
Moderately slow	160	325	3
Moderate	180 - 190	350 - 375	4
Moderately hot	200 - 210	400 - 425	5
Hot	220 - 230	450 - 475	6
Very hot	240 - 250	500 - 525	7

Life's easier with these great Home Library gifts

Protect your favourite cookbooks and keep them clean, tidy and within easy reach with this smart vinyl folder. PLUS you can follow our recipes perfectly with a set of measuring cups and spoons, as used in the Women's Weekly Test Kitchen.

TO ORDER YOUR BOOK HOLDER OR MEASURING SET:

Price: Book Holder $11.95 (Australia); elsewhere $A21.95.
Metric Measuring Set $5.95 (Australia); $A8.00 (New Zealand); $A9.95 elsewhere
prices include postage and handling. This offer is available in all countries.

Phone: Have your credit card details ready. Sydney: (02) 9260 0035; **elsewhere in Australia:** 1800 252 515 (free call, Mon-Fri, 8.30am-5.30pm) or FAX your order to (02) 9267 4363 or MAIL your order by photocopying or completing the coupon below.

Payment: **Australian residents:** we accept the credit cards listed, money orders and cheques. **Overseas residents:** we accept the credit cards listed, drafts in $A drawn on an Australian bank, and also English, New Zealand and U.S. cheques in the currency of the country of issue. Credit card charges are at the exchange rate current at the time of payment.

Complete coupon and fax or post to:
AWW Home Library Reader Offer, ACP Direct, PO Box 7036, Sydney NSW 1028.